Hem

Please renew or return items by the date shown on your receipt

www.hertsdirect.org/libraries

Renewals and enquiries: 0300 123 4049

Textphone for hearing or speech impaired   0300 123 4041

Hertfordshire

Vanishing London

© Haynes Publishing, 2011

The right of Paul Joseph to be identified as the author of this Work has been asserted
by him in accordance with the Copyright, Designs & Patents Act 1988.

First published in 2011

A catalogue record for this book is available from the British Library

ISBN: 978-0-857330-38-3

Published by Haynes Publishing, Sparkford, Yeovil,
Somerset BA22 7JJ, UK
Tel: 01963 442030 Fax: 01963 440001
Int. tel: +44 1963 442030 Int. fax: +44 1963 440001
E-mail: sales@haynes.co.uk
Website: www.haynes.co.uk

Haynes North America Inc., 861 Lawrence Drive,
Newbury Park, California 91320, USA

All images © Mirrorpix

Creative Director: Kevin Gardner
Designed for Haynes by BrainWave

Printed and bound in the US

Vanishing London

THE PLACES · THE PEOPLE · THE STORIES

Paul Joseph

FOREWORD BY Robert Elms

Contents

Foreword

There's an old saying, which suggests that "London will be a great city when it's finished." But of course the reality is precisely the opposite. London, this unruly, unknowable metropolis, a monstrous, many-headed Hydra of a city in a constant state of flux would really be finished if it were ever finished. What has given London such a unique appeal is the way in which it constantly reinvents itself, shedding skins and adopting guises as each generation puts their stamp on this ever-evolving organism.

Yet for all London's ability to be perpetually born again, nothing ever quite dies here. The ghosts of 2,000 years of continual habitation, of all those Londons which have gone before, can still be found lurking in the many layers of the city. Walk down that alley, through that arch or over that bridge and suddenly you are immersed in a different era or another facet. Turn a corner and you have gone from Georgian to modern, bomb damaged to designer glamorous, the character of an area changing dramatically as you cross a single street. The juxtaposition of old and new, beautiful and ugly, traditional and radical, virtuous and venal is what makes London so unique.

Londoners too are a contradictory lot, proud of their town but prone to moaning, cultured yet unpretentious, ordered and patient in queues yet known to flare up into protest and riot, by turns patriotic and anarchic. It is surely only in London that the twin worlds of arch-conservatism of court and queen, pomp and ceremony could coexist so successfully with the cutting-edge creativity of punk and pop, rave and style. This complex city is simultaneously deeply traditional and amazingly trendy.

And since the invention of photography London has been a willing sitter for so many gifted thieves of light, lenses trained on the fleeting and the eternal alike, capturing moments and freezing motion. It has been blitzed and bombed, slum-cleared and town-planned, it's been the epicentre of ever-changing youth movements and the bastion of unchanging ritual, as it's moved from the heart of empire to bustling multiculturalism, from post-war austerity through swinging creativity, from grey and foggy to bright and technicolour. We've seen the working docks replaced by the high-rise towers of commerce, trolleybuses and trams superseded by the now-lamented Routemasters, street markets decline and revive, whole neighbourhoods shift from rich to poor and back again. And it's all been recorded.

Much has vanished from chameleon London, more perhaps than from any other major city, but because of these shots it is not truly gone. And London of course goes on, a perpetual work in progress.

Robert Elms

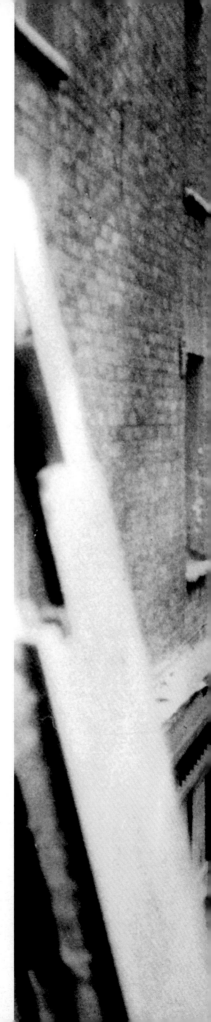

Introduction

Growing up in Greater London in the 1980s, living in the kind of semi-detached dwelling that had come to dominate the post-war suburban landscape, a trip into the city centre held a glamorous allure. In the naivety of childhood, little did I appreciate the nexus between the city's inner and outer confines. The increased social mobility, new housing policies and extensive developments in transport that had created the impetus for a mass-movement of people to what became known as London's "commuter belt", was beyond my comprehension.

I was a new breed of Londoner: consigned to its edges, a downgraded member of a venerable club. My perception of the city was, whether I knew it or not, being shaped from the outside looking in.

It was in this spirit of detached reflection that I set about researching this book. With the native Londoner increasingly becoming a relic of the past, it seemed to represent vanishing London in an intangible microcosm. When a church, or pub, or cinema is demolished, we are left with a physical reminder of its departure. But what happens to the Londoner when they are no longer of this city? Do they remain imbued with London's spirit, or is this nothing more than trite sentimentality?

As the joke goes, nostalgia ain't what it used to be. Yet there is little doubt that in recent years there has been a surge of interest in people delving into the past, to relive, celebrate or simply lament a bygone era. It is evidenced in retro fashion boutiques, themed club nights, social history documentaries, classic movies, vintage cars...

Perhaps it is a response to our discomfort at these fast-moving times. The techno-revolution has impacted on every facet of life, making it almost impossible to keep pace with changing trends and innovations. Could it be that nostalgia acts as a sedative to help us cope with the world's relentless march forwards?

One thing is certain: London is an immensely different place to 30, 40, 50 or 100 years ago. Its rich and tumultuous history has left a melange of architectural features and cultural and social milieus. As I began to probe Mirrorpix's extensive archive of historical photography, its value as a resource to explore the London that has been left behind became glaringly clear.

I ploughed through the goldmine of material, and it struck me how each photograph resonated at once with both a familiarity and a profound sense of change. I hope that this book stimulates a similar sharpness of emotion in its readers, whether born within earshot of the Bow Bells, or somewhere beyond.

Paul Joseph, author of Vanishing London

Majestic
Metropolis

The 20th century saw heavy regeneration across vast swathes of London, but the foundations of the city's streetscapes continue to bear hallmarks of yesteryear. Remnants of both Georgian and Victorian London linger beyond the contemporary facades of many buildings, whilst those with a sharp historical eye can even find vestiges of medieval times.

Nevertheless, significant cosmetic changes have inexorably lent a new texture to much of London's topography. The catalyst for redevelopment has often been commercialism, but more benevolent forces have also contributed to the city's urban evolution. Not least the city's dynamic cultural scene, whose artists have helped transform several London districts from nondescript, run-down areas into vibrant, bohemian melting pots.

"Architecturally, London may be said to represent chaos itself"

Percy Hunter, 1885

ABOVE: A floodlit St Paul's Cathedral during Victory in Europe celebrations, May 1945.

What Goes Up Must Come Down

London has never been a cohesive city. Having accumulated its buildings over such a long period of time it has always been a hotchpotch of architectural styles.

In this perpetually evolving city, Londoners are all too accustomed to its ever-changing appearance, often to the point of indifference. Whether destroyed by war, neglect, or in the name of modernity, many of the city's edifices have been erased from our memory almost as completely as they have been erased from the physical spaces they once occupied.

The driving force for change has always varied according to the financial, political, cultural and architectural atmosphere of the era. In Victorian London, Britain's newly acquired imperial status saw much of the city's Georgian, Shakespearean and medieval heritage demolished and replaced by statement-making stone edifices more in keeping with the nation's global standing.

Redevelopment in 20th century London was more typically an expression of a new and pervasive architectural spirit. In an unmistakable nod to the skyscrapers of America, the city took on an increasingly jagged appearance. Tall office blocks merged into the city's historic street patterns to create a unique and highly concentrated visual mixture of old and new. The trend skywards is illustrated by the fact that London's tallest building at the end of the 20th century – the Canary Wharf tower – was more than double the height of the tallest at the beginning of the century – St Paul's Cathedral.

The city's modern fondness for high-rise architecture has not only led to the disappearance of several old buildings, but also threatened some of London's most classic sight lines. In response, traditionalists have fought for legislation to prevent popular landmarks being blocked from view. Currently there are 10 sight lines to St Paul's Cathedral from around the capital that enjoy legal protection, including the 10-mile view from Richmond Park, as well as vantage points in Hampstead and Greenwich.

Where Londoners live has risen skywards, too. In the immediate post-war years, the vast amount of homes destroyed by German bombs, coupled with a national baby boom that sent the population spiralling, made housing a major issue. To tackle the problem, the authorities decided on the creation of space-saving, high-rise flats.

London's skyline dramatically altered as these functional tower blocks were erected across previously low-rise urban areas. In some districts, Victorian slums that had survived the war were knocked down and replaced with tracts of social housing. Away from the centre, the M4 motorway swept through west London clearing away swathes of old terraced housing in its path. Meanwhile, a policy was introduced to encourage people to move into newly built towns surrounding the capital.

As Londoners have migrated out from the city borders and into the suburbs and rural hinterland, the first line of defence in the fight to retain the cityscape is a dedicated troupe of conservationists and community activists offering a counterweight against the relentless pursuit of "progress" – on occasion with great success. In 1973 Covent Garden Market was saved from destruction, whilst Piccadilly Circus and south Soho have also survived numerous redevelopment schemes. Elsewhere, having been earmarked for demolition in the mid-Sixties, the grandiose St Pancras station succeeded not only in being saved from dereliction but also restored to its original iron-and-glass glory.

At other times, however, the efforts of the conservationists and activists have been in vain. In the mid-20th century, the property tycoon Joe Levy created a canyon of high-rise office blocks along Euston Road, sweeping away the old Victorian Euston station in the process. A victim of this demolition work was the Euston Arch, a symbol of London's lost architecture, which features later in this book. The magnificent Greek Revival gateway fronted Euston station in Central London between 1837 and 1961. It was a triumphant structure, and an emblem of the grand British railways. Yet in spite of a vigorous campaign to save it, the Arch was pulled down in the interests of the modernization of the railways. The fight against its demise was led by leading figures in the field of architectural history, but its fate was sealed by politicians who cast it off as a non-functional object that couldn't be allowed to impede the city's march towards a vague and intangible vision of a better future.

There is an argument that the lost architecture of London should not be mourned too deeply, so often has it represented grinding poverty and social breakdown. But many still feel a sense of regret for the demise of buildings and public spaces that offered a link to the city's historical past.

ABOVE: This photo shows Trafalgar Square in May 1937. The two lily-shaped stone-basin fountains that can be seen below Nelson's Column were replaced two years later by the distinctive variations that flank the square today.

LEFT: An aerial view of the Maritime Greenwich world heritage site, south east London, August 1958. Visible are the Cutty Sark ship, a merchant vessel built in 1869, and the Old Royal Naval College.

13

Remnants of Medieval London

The medieval period was one of huge flux in London. The largest and wealthiest city in England it may have been, but it was also primitive and its citizens were at the mercy of foul diseases due to poor sanitation. Regular fires in the cramped confines of the city meant that construction of new buildings was a perpetual sight. Incredibly, some of the edifices of the era still remain, albeit only visible in their architectural minutiae.

BELOW: This black-and-white, half-timbered structure overlooking High Holborn is one of London's few surviving Tudor buildings. It dates from 1586 when it began life as a wool staple, where wool was weighed and taxed.

London's Unyielding Churches

London's centuries-old churches have seen it all over the years. The Great Fire of London and two World Wars have furnished the city's places of worship with an endless supply of dinner-party anecdotes. Alas, many did not survive to tell the tales. Wartime bombings and a spate of 19th-century demolitions took their toll and reduced the number of churches that were once prevalent across the city landscape. Most of those that remain have undergone facelifts due to varying levels of wear and tear – but they continue to offer one of the most resonant links to London's past.

LEFT: St Clement Danes Church, located on the Strand. The church, which was designed by Sir Christopher Wren in the late 17th century, was virtually destroyed during the Blitz before undergoing major restoration during the post-war years.

BELOW: St Martin-in-the-Field Church, seen from the entrance to the National Portrait Gallery on St Martin's Place off Trafalgar Square, circa 1960s.

Throughout the 20th century, negotiating London's major junctions and thoroughfares has been a case of "survival of the fittest". Pedestrians, horses and vehicles alike have engaged in a free-for-all on roads originally laid out by Romans some 1,600 years ago. That the city has continued to function despite these antiquated foundations is something of a miracle.

LEFT: A busy cross-road at Elephant and Castle, circa 1905.

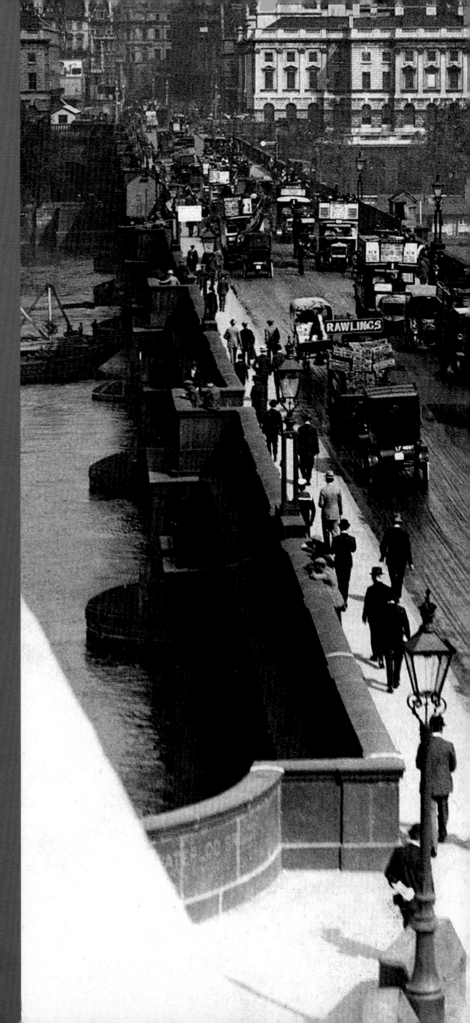

RIGHT: Traffic crossing the River Thames on the old Waterloo Bridge, December 1925. The bridge was closed as unsafe in 1923, and replaced with a temporary structure that can be seen here. Work began on a replacement bridge in 1937, but, having been interrupted by the Second World War, it did not officially open until 1945.

OPPOSITE: Traffic on Regent Street, November 1959.

BELOW: The Embankment jammed with traffic during the General Strike of May 1926.

OPPOSITE: Oxford Circus looking east, circa 1938.

BELOW: The junction of Tottenham Court Road and St Giles Circus, August 1934.

RIGHT: A street scene on the
Hammersmith Bridge Road, west London,
circa 1910.

The Evolution of Trafalgar Square

Until the mid-19th century, Trafalgar Square was a sparse and unremarkable site in the heart of Central London. But over the course of 30 years the area in and around the Square was transformed by the addition of several features that would become some of London's most iconic landmarks. The construction of the National Gallery in 1838, Nelson's Column in 1843, two stone-basin fountains in 1845 and four bronze lions in 1867 created a distinctiveness that made the Square an ideal social meeting place, as well as a centre of national democracy and protest.

In July 2003 another vast construction project was completed that involved the pedestrianization of the north side of the Square, as well as several other changes designed to improve accessibility to the National Gallery and provide the public with better facilities. As a consequence the entire atmosphere of the Square has changed. The removal of traffic from one side has lent a new calm to the area and for the first time it can now truly be called a public space.

LEFT AND ABOVE: Two views of Trafalgar Square from different eras and angles. The main photo shows the square busy with horse-drawn transport, with the National Gallery in the background, circa 1900. The smaller photo is shot from between the National Gallery (left) and South Africa House (right), July 1953.

Where's Eros?

Sharp-eyed readers may notice two discrepancies in the photo opposite of Piccadilly Circus, taken in 1946. Firstly, conspicuous by their absence are the Shaftesbury Monument Memorial Fountain and the Eros statue, usually found sitting on top. The monument had been covered and the statue removed during the Second World War to protect them from bombing raids. Secondly, the position of the base, sitting here in the centre of the Circus, will have alerted some. During the late 1980s, the entire fountain was moved from the centre to the south-west side, where it stands today.

ABOVE: A bus advertising Johnnie Walker whisky passes through Piccadilly Circus, circa 1925.

OPPOSITE: Piccadilly Circus, 1946.

OPPOSITE INSET: Eros is returned home in June 1947.

The Big Smoke

It is not just transport that has interrupted London's flow. Since Roman times, the city has experienced spells of large-scale mist and fog – often dubbed "pea-soupers". However, the London smog of 1952 had unprecedented consequences.

In early December that year, a dense smoke-filled fog shrouded London and brought the city to a standstill. For four days, cars were routinely abandoned, trains were disrupted and airports closed. The smog also seeped indoors: at Sadler's Wells Theatre in Islington, the opera *La Traviata* had to be abandoned after the first act due to lack of visibility.

But there was also a substantial human cost. A Ministry of Health report estimated that 4,000 people had died due to respiratory or cardiovascular problems during the outbreak. In response to the events, the government passed several changes in legislation, including the Clean Air Act 1956. The battle for better air quality in London continues, but a time when smog could overwhelm the city as it did in 1952 is now a distant memory.

"In London, above all what I love is the fog" Monet

TOP: A policeman on point duty uses flares to guide London traffic during a heavy smog, December 1952.

ABOVE: Traffic crawling along in the London smog, circa 1960s.

OPPOSITE: A high gas holder at Southall covered by fog in the Thames Valley, 1949.

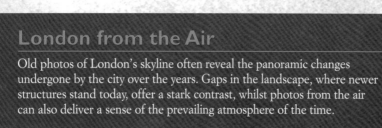

London from the Air

Old photos of London's skyline often reveal the panoramic changes undergone by the city over the years. Gaps in the landscape, where newer structures stand today, offer a stark contrast, whilst photos from the air can also deliver a sense of the prevailing atmosphere of the time.

LEFT: The Graf Zeppelin German airship passes over London during a 21,500-mile round-the-world trip, April 1930.

RIGHT: An aerial view of the River Thames. The photo was taken east looking south in August 1958, and will be pleasing to fans of London's bridges. The five on show, from the bottom, are Tower Bridge, London Bridge, Cannon Street Railway Bridge, Southwark Bridge and Blackfriars Bridge. The one addition to the riverscape has been the Millennium Bridge, located between Southwark and Blackfriars bridges, which opened in June 2000.

LEFT: The photo here, taken in August 1959, is dominated by St Paul's Cathedral, but surrounding it are some notable additions to the cityscape: office blocks constructed during the post-war economic boom.

River Thames: London's Veins

Whilst the Thames has been a constant feature throughout London's history, other rivers have fallen by the wayside. The most prominent was the Fleet, which flowed through a large valley between Ludgate Hill and Holborn. Its primary use was also the cause of its demise – with market traders regularly depositing excrement and dead animals into its waters. The authorities eventually lost patience in their efforts to prevent such practices and the entire river was bricked over in the mid-19th century.

TOP: Port of London Dock Guides on the River Thames in London, 1965.
ABOVE: Barges on the River Thames with docks and warehouses in the background, circa 1946.
OPPOSITE: A dramatic, above cloud-level aspect of the Port of London and the Thames from 8,000 feet, circa 1935.

London's Bridges

London's river crossings have been some of the more resilient of the city's features, enabling both commercial and leisure pursuits for centuries. Today, there are 24 bridges that span the River Thames – the oldest being London Bridge, which dates back to the 12th century and, for more than six centuries, remained the river's only crossing.

Originally made from wood, London Bridge was replaced by a stone structure at the start of the 13th century, allowing for the construction of houses and shops along its sides. The road itself was so narrow that it often jammed with pedestrians, horses and carts. In 1733 a "keep left" rule was enforced to keep the traffic moving, eventually becoming the rule of the road in Britain.

In 1757 the houses and shops on the bridge were demolished, and a new granite bridge was built in its place in 1831. This lasted until 1973 when concrete was used to construct the iconic structure that we know today.

ABOVE: "Mad Major" Christopher Draper, an English flying ace of the First World War, flying under Westminster Bridge in an Auster aircraft, 1953.

OPPOSITE: Tower Bridge, circa 1950s.

RIGHT: Albert Bridge in west London, circa 1985.

Cathedrals of the Railway

Just as the Thames has facilitated the movement of people and goods across London and beyond, so have the city's railways. The grandiose stations that thousands pass through each day are testament to the city's ability to combine function with beauty.

ABOVE: The Euston Arch covered in scaffolding, circa 1960. The arch formed the entrance to Euston train station until it was demolished in 1961 as part of wider refurbishment. Its destruction was contested by a fierce campaign that in recent years has come to prominence once again, led by the Euston Arch Trust, that advocates the rebuilding of "one of London's lost masterpieces".

LEFT: A view of Euston Road outside St Pancras station, September 1931.

RIGHT: Sunlight streams through the windows of Liverpool Street station, circa 1970.

BELOW: Queen Mary opening Waterloo station in March 1922.

Post-war Poverty

Much of London's slum areas were destroyed during the Second World War and rebuilt as a higher standard of accommodation, mainly through council house provision. However, some slums remained as a blot on the urban landscape and a reminder of London's enduring social deprivation.

ABOVE: Ramshackle houses in London, documented to highlight the plight of many families living in slum dwellings, circa 1960.

RIGHT: Three families share a two-bedroom terraced house in Paddington, meaning that one family must sleep in the kitchen, October 1953.

"Poverty never leaves London. It merely changes its form and appearance" Peter Ackroyd

Metro-land

In 1903, Pinner was the first London suburb to benefit from the creation of a housing estate by the Metropolitan Railway, a company set up to develop housing and shops along the Metropolitan railway line. Such enterprises proliferated in the first quarter of the century, as railway advancements made commuting from provincial areas into Central London quick and reliable. The term "Metro-land" was coined to describe these areas that spanned the counties of Buckinghamshire, Hertfordshire and Middlesex. The slogan "Live in Metro-land" was even etched on the door handles of Metropolitan train carriages. Metro-land was designed to ease the crowds of the city centre, but inevitably, as the suburbs grew, they too became congested. Playing 'sardines' on the commute home is a game familiar to all Londoners.

ABOVE: Commuters queue to get home outside a suburban tube station, circa 1946.

LEFT: A newspaper advert for a housing estate in the north-west London suburb of Pinner, 1935.

PINNER VILLAGE ESTATE and RIDGEWAY ESTATE
(NORTH HARROW)
Attached to Harrow's finest recreation park of 26 acres.

SPECIAL terms to Civil Servants, Bank, Insurance and Railway Officials. For 25 years the name 'Cutlers' has stood for high quality and sound value. 2,300 houses built in this district. We welcome inspection by your own surveyor or building expert. Two sales out of every five are the direct result of recommendations by satisfied owners.
Garage space to all types. In Metroland —20 minutes from Town. No road charges or law costs.

POST COUPON AT ONCE ➤

Enquirers will not be called upon by canvassers unless requested.

Type "D.B." £695 Freehold
Semi-det. Bungalows £650 (16/8 weekly). Detached Bungalows £695 (17/10 weekly) as illustrated. Semi-det. Houses from £735 (19/1 weekly). Detached Houses £935 and £975. With 2/3rds loan, low interest at 3½% and reduced weekly payments.

CUTLERS LTD
62 Station Rd.   North Harrow
'Phone: Harrow 0140 (3 lines)

Please send free travelling voucher from Baker Street, and booklet.

Name..................................
Address..............................
D.M. 16/11/35

The Master Builder

Hungarian-born architect Ernö Goldfinger rose to prominence in England after the Second World War when the country was faced with the task of replacing the 4 million houses that had been destroyed during wartime bombing raids. The government saw high-rise buildings as a solution, and Goldfinger's skill at designing tower blocks soon elevated him to a position of national distinction.

Goldfinger was, however, a controversial and eccentric figure. His Brutalist style of architecture – typically using concrete with repetitive angular geometries – was disliked by many, whilst his eccentricity was illustrated by his fondness for "sampling" his buildings by temporarily taking residence in them. For two months in 1968, he and his wife moved into Flat 130 on the 25th floor at Balfron Tower in east London, where they threw champagne parties to find out what other residents thought of his design.

ABOVE: Consort House, a block of luxury apartments in Queensway, Bayswater, July 1970.

OPPOSITE: Ernö Goldfinger in front of the Balfron Tower high-rise flats that he designed in Poplar, east London, February 1968. The building was given Grade II listed status in 1996. In 2007, it was agreed by consent between residents and the council that a full refurbishment of the tower would take place, bringing it up to modern living standards.

Working
London

London's status as a global trading centre dates back to the 19th century, when the city was the capital of the British Empire. Many of the industries of that time have endured, such as the still-thriving market trade, but advancements in machinery have unalterably transformed some working practices, including newspaper production.

There are some occupations that have simply disappeared altogether. The London Docks, once the largest port in the world and a symbol of the city's industrial potency, employed an army of workers until it closed to shipping in the 1960s. Meanwhile, the enchanting image of the rag-and-bone man and his horse-drawn cart on London's streets has also been consigned to history.

"London has always been established on the imperatives of money and of trade"

Peter Ackroyd

LEFT: Porters near to Billingsgate fish market in the City of London, circa 1935.

Trading Places

Throughout the 20th century, the changing nature of employment in London has run parallel with its evolving role as a world city.

At the start of the century London was the biggest and most prosperous metropolis the world had ever known. One hundred years later, most of its manufacturing industry has been lost and it has fallen behind several other urban centres across the globe in terms of wealth, population and potential.

Working life in London has almost completely changed over the past 100 years. Manual skills have been replaced by machinery, regulation has improved working conditions, and fewer people stay with the same employer for long periods of time. Many jobs are simply not required anymore: the working practices of lamplighters, switchboard operators, button makers, bus conductors and newspaper print setters, to name just a few, have all been transferred from human to automatic operation.

Some of the biggest changes to working life in London have been felt by the city's female population. The First World War gave vast numbers of women their first experience of male-dominated professions, serving as replacements for the men involved in the war effort. While many men returned to their jobs after the war, in certain professions the reversal was permanent. Before long, women began to outnumber men in secretarial, administrative and shop work, casting off their traditional roles as home-workers or in domestic-service jobs.

The default option for most women without an obvious career path was to become a secretary. However, the computerization of the office environment and the increased use of IT among senior staff eventually reduced the need for traditional secretarial skills. In the 1990s, Pitman's Secretarial College on Southampton Row, Central London – the institution where so many women down the years had learned their shorthand and typewriting skills – closed its doors for the last time.

As well as the substantial changes in working practices following the First World War, the years that followed the end of the Second World War saw work patterns change across London once again. In the 1950s London witnessed a boom in its motor, aviation and building industries as the city was redeveloped following the damage inflicted by German bombs. Also thriving were the expansive London docks, which were now employing some 30,000 men.

By the 1960s, however, the British Empire was fading and the aftershocks were being felt across London's industrial landscape. Newly independent countries began trading elsewhere, threatening the stranglehold London had enjoyed for so long through its status as the capital and heartbeat of the empire.

Another important change took place in 1973 when Britain joined the European Economic Community (EEC). This had a further impact on London's ability to compete on the global industrial stage, as imports from Commonwealth countries became limited by new quotas and tariffs.

The London docks, whose trade tended to come from the Commonwealth, felt the pinch as much as any industry. In an effort to cut costs, the Docks Authority moved to cheaper containerized facilities at Tilbury in Essex, but many of the old docks were forced to close. Other industries with close connections to the docks, such as sugar refining and food processing, were also hit hard.

Around the same period came the demise of one of London's industrial monoliths, the Beckton Gas Works, located in East Ham. One of the world's largest gas facilities, it was forced to close in 1969 after the discovery of natural gas in the North Sea.

Within six years another of the city's major landmarks had joined the ranks of defunct industrial buildings when Battersea Power Station was decommissioned. Spiralling operating costs and increased understanding of the damage inflicted by sulphur emissions from the station were the cause of its downfall, though the building itself still stands as a much-loved reminder of London's Art Deco heritage.

As London entered the 1970s, the factory system that had emerged in Britain with the Industrial Revolution had fallen into decline. Advancements in technology had reduced the need for hands-on manufacturing methods, whilst increased competition overseas reduced the profitability of these traditional workhouses. They began to close in increasing numbers across London and beyond.

By the 1980s many of the manufacturing industries that had boomed for decades had either declined or fallen away completely. London was still a working city, but its ways and means of working had changed forever.

Keeping London Working

Away from the 'shop floor' of London's markets and retail landscape, the city continues to function thanks to the toil of hardy individuals prepared to get their hands dirty for minimal reward. Today we take our comforts and privileges – including sanitary conditions – for granted, but it was not ever thus.

During the 19th century, the urgency for a modern, sanitary sewage system was increased by the Great Stink of 1858, when the pungent smell of untreated sewage overwhelmed large parts of Central London. In response, a civil engineer called Joseph Bazalgette was charged with designing an extensive underground system that diverted waste to the Thames Estuary, away from the city's main populated areas. Further plans to increase the carrying capacity of London's sewerage system were debated for some years, and were finally confirmed in 2007.

ABOVE: A sewer man pictured below London's streets, December 1969.

LEFT: Workmen cleaning the face of Big Ben, May 1953.

The Rag-and-bone Man

The photos on this page show the evolution of a famous and charming old trading practice that saw labourers collect unwanted junk from its owners. Below shows the traditional rag-and-bone man traversing a cobbled London street with a horse-drawn cart, whilst opposite sees the transition to automotive transport – in this case a pickup truck. However, social changes, such as the increased tendency for all members of a household to work outside the home, made casual street-by-street pickup unworkable, and the trade in its original form has now disappeared.

Tradesman Exit

Londoners have never been afraid to get their hands dirty. The popular image of the soot-faced chimney sweep is part of our vision of a Dickensian London. The hardy profession came into being during the early years of the Industrial Revolution as chimneys became large enough for a person to fit inside. Despite their old-fashioned characteristics, workmen such as chimney sweeps, blacksmiths and locksmiths still ply their trade in the capital today.

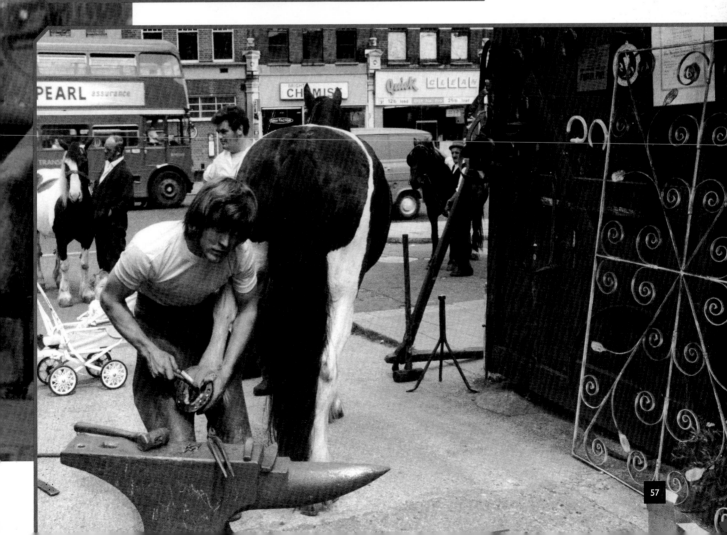

OPPOSITE: A horse stops for refreshments from its job of pulling coal through the streets of London, June 1955.

LEFT: A London chimney sweep with his brush and rods, circa 1937.

BELOW: A blacksmith at work in Brent, north-west London, July 1970.

Temples of Trade

London is proud of its inimitable market culture. But whilst many of its markets date back to medieval times, some have not stood up to the 21st century, suffering a variation of disrepair, displacement and commercial development. In 1982, Billingsgate fish market, famous for the coarse language of its traders, relocated to a new building complex close to Canary Wharf in the Docklands, east London. The previous building, known as Old Billingsgate Market, is now used as a corporate events venue. In 2005, a review of London's wholesale markets left a question mark hanging over the future of Billingsgate that remains today. The review centred on the question of whether it would be better to have a smaller number of markets all selling a full range of fresh produce, rather than separate specialist markets.

Only Smithfield has remained in the city centre. The huge meat market has retained its ancient working practices, though it too has seen the encroachment of the 20th century: the onset of Mad Cow Disease coupled with deadly E Coli bacteria strains have seen it modernized in recent times – shedding the market of much of its distinctive character. Additionally, like its Billingsgate counterpart, Smithfield has been under threat of demolition in recent years, as plans to replace it with office blocks were put forward. However, the proposals were shelved after government intervention and the market's immediate future appears safe.

OPPOSITE: Porters outside Billingsgate
Fish Market, circa 1950s.

LEFT: A fire blazes at Smithfield Meat
Market, January 1958.

LEFT: London's oldest street market, the Caledonian Market in Islington, north London, circa 1920s. Originally a cattle market, at the start of the 20th century it became a bric-a-brac market after the cattle trade diminished, and became notorious for its sale of stolen goods. It closed after the Second World War and relocated to Bermondsey, south London. Today the site is occupied by public housing estates, sports pitches and a park.

BELOW: An aerial view of Petticoat Lane Market, which traditionally sells clothes, in east London, December 1950.

Fleet Street

One of the curiosities of London is what the eminent London author Peter Ackroyd describes as the city's "territorial imperative". This geographical quirk has seen both trades and communities dominating specific areas of the city, uninterrupted by demographic or economic shifts.

For nearly three centuries, Fleet Street in Central London was the de facto home of the English newspaper industry. By the mid-20th century, the imposing thoroughfare boasted the headquarters of virtually every major daily newspaper in the country. By day the street buzzed with the machinations of journalism – including an infamous pub culture – and by night it hummed to the sound of the printing press.

However, in the final quarter of the century, the majestic old buildings that housed these national mouthpieces began struggling to keep pace with the demands of technology. The 1980s saw most of the papers relocate, with Australian media tycoon Rupert Murdoch leading the charge by moving his own newspapers to Wapping in Tower Hamlets. Others set up camp in the heart of London's Docklands, in the centrepiece Canary Wharf tower.

Today Fleet Street is more associated with the industries of banking and law. But in one sense its legacy lives on, with the name of the street remaining shorthand for England's newspaper business.

ABOVE LEFT: Large rolls of paper being delivered to the *Daily Mirror*'s printing house on Bouverie Street in the City of London, March 1905.

LEFT: A modern printing press is demonstrated at the London School of Printing and Kindred Trades in Elephant and Castle, south London, circa 1950. The building now houses the London College of Communication.

OPPOSITE: The *Daily Mirror* building decorated to celebrate VJ day to mark the end of the Second World War.

London's waterways were once at the heart of the city's trade and industry. In previous centuries the River Thames was permanently clogged with ships from across the world and at one time London boasted more shipyards than anywhere on earth. The London Docks, built in 1815, were its main trading post, dealing in products such as timber, grain, wool, sugar and rubber.

German bombing during the Second World War caused huge damage to the docks, leaving substantial rebuilding required. Despite a resurgence during the 1950s, the Docks eventually succumbed to advancements in cargo transportation following the introduction of a newly invented container system. The 30-acre site could no longer accommodate the size of vessels required and the shipping industry moved to deep-water ports outside of London.

Between 1960 and 1980, all of London's docks were closed, leaving around eight square miles of derelict land. When Margaret Thatcher came to power in the 1980s, she decided to use the prime chunk of real estate to redevelop the Docks as a second financial hub – a rival to the Square Mile. From this vision came the modern day Docklands we see today, where the old world of ships, wharves, cranes and warehouses has been replaced by offices, shops, wine bars and exclusive apartments.

LEFT: A view of the Thames with the Pool of London on the right and Tower Bridge in the distance, September 1935. The Pool of London was an important conduit in the functioning of the Port of London until the entire area was demolished during the 1960s.

OPPOSITE: Tower Bridge, August 1939. The closure of the London Docks in 1969 led to a massive reduction in river traffic. Today the bridge is raised four or five times a week compared to 50 times a day in its heyday.

ABOVE: The gateway to the East India Dock railway station in Poplar, east London, August 1911. The station closed in 1944 after Second World War bombing.

OPPOSITE: An aerial view of the London Docks during a five-week dockers' strike, April 1975.

Covent Garden

Having originally been the arable land and orchard for Westminster Abbey the area known as Covent Garden was rebuilt as a fashionable square in the late 16th century. By 1654 a small fruit and vegetable market had been established on the square's south side which expanded through the 18th century, as well as becoming a red-light district. By 1830 the Neo-classical building had been erected to help organize the market. By the 1960s the traffic congestion had become so bad that the market had to be found a new home and in 1974 the sale of fruit and vegetables moved to the New Covent Garden at Nine Elms, south of the River Thames. This picture was taken in 1946.

Disused but not Forgotten

The history of London's power supply system prior to the inauguration of the national grid is one of diversity and, arguably, gross inefficiency. At one time the city had over 70 separate power stations, with many barely registering on the public consciousness.

One that certainly did, and continues to leave its mark, is Battersea Power Station in south London. The photo below, taken in 1951, shows Station A. A few years later, Station B was added to the east of the original structure, providing the four-chimney layout that remains today. Station A was decommissioned in 1975 and Station B followed in 1983. The Art Deco edifice has remained one of London's most distinctive landmarks and is still the largest brick building in Europe. It was awarded Grade II listed status in 1980, and Grade II* status in 2007.

ABOVE: Lots Road Power Station in Chelsea, west London, circa 1923. When built it was the largest power station in the world, and supplied power to the London Underground network. The station was decommissioned in 2002 and plans to convert the site into shops, restaurants and apartments were approved in 2006.

OPPOSITE: Battersea Power Station (Station A), illuminated at night during the Festival of Britain, May 1951.

Adding Value to London

The illuminated advertising in Piccadilly Circus is a kaleidoscopic icon of London. The first signs arrived in 1910 and were initially met with disapproval by many who considered them tawdry and gimmicky. London authorities initially tried to exert some control over the quality of the adverts, but the city's commercial imperative prevailed.

For the first half of the century the dominant adverts in Piccadilly were for British drinks' companies Bovril and Schweppes. In the 1920s the Irish stout Guinness ran an advertising campaign using the slogan "Guinness is Good for You", which stemmed from market research revealing people felt "good" after drinking it. In later years as regulations over public health became more scrupulous, Guinness was forced to stop using the slogan.

But changes in the nature of Piccadilly's famous adverts have not only been led by social developments. Globalization has also played its part. By the second half of the 20th century Coca-Cola and other multinational firms had taken over the area's elevated advertising spaces. Such firms included Japanese electrical corporations – something that would have been unthinkable in the immediacy of the Second World War.

RIGHT: The neon signs visible in Piccadilly Circus, advertising home-made British products including Bovril, Schweppes and Guinness, May 1945. The crowds surrounding the covered plinth are celebrating VE Day.

The Demise of the High Street

During the past 25 years, many of London's independent stores have been forced out of business as a homogenized retail landscape has emerged in their place. This change has been driven by a combination of shifting market forces and the increasing power and convenience of the Internet.

Major supermarkets have led this new monopoly, with their ability to undercut their smaller counterparts by offering cheaper goods. The Internet, meanwhile, has impacted most heavily on the book and music sectors. High-profile examples in recent years include the disappearance of high street institutions Our Price and Woolworths, owing largely to the shrinking of the demand for physical copies of music, and the ability to purchase them from home.

Effects on the book industry have been equally acute. Certainly, if you bought this humble tome in a store, you will have participated in a dying trade, since most people now buy their books online. The recent arrival of e-books is expected to further diminish the need for high street bookstores.

OPPOSITE ABOVE: A Soho bookshop, December 1970.

OPPOSITE BELOW: Customers peruse books in an open window of Foyles bookshop on Charing Cross Road, October 1957. First opened in 1903, it was once in the *Guinness Book of Records* as the world's largest bookstore. Whilst it has so far survived the general decline of the book trade, it is far removed from the store it once was. Previously known for its eccentric and antiquated business practices, the store modernized at the end of the century. However, its penchant for bucking the trend remains evident in its sale of second-hand and out-of-print books.

RIGHT: A newspaper advert for Woolworths' high-street retail chain, 1980. In 2008/09, all 807 UK stores closed as the chain succumbed to a decade of decline.

BELOW: A woman buying a packet of cigarettes in a tobacconist shop in London, June 1940. As requested by the sign on the counter, the customer leaves a spare cigarette in a collection box, which will be sent on to a hospital for wounded Second World War soldiers. Today, the tobacconist's is a trade under threat, with only a handful remaining across London.

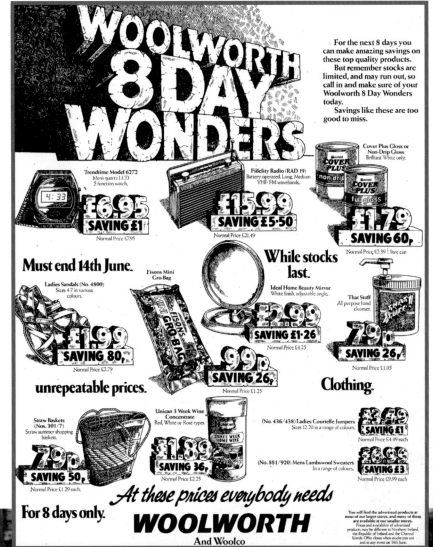

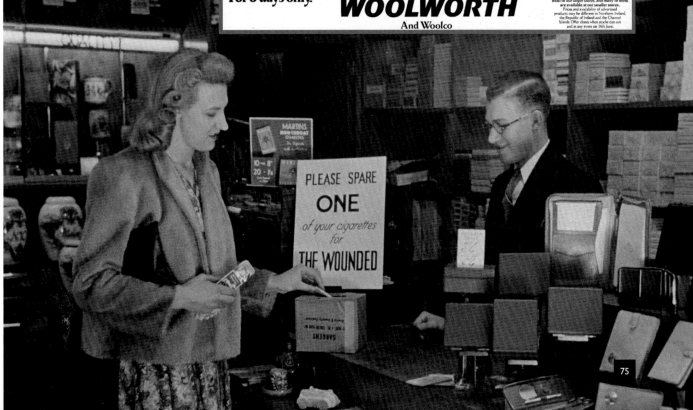

Urban Playground

Many of the leisure activities pursued by Londoners a century ago have stood the test of time, but are now enjoyed in a modernized form, often led by technological innovations and cultural shifts. Live entertainment remains as popular as ever, but the sites in which Londoners have gone to be entertained have not always survived. A large number of cinemas and theatre halls have either been demolished or undergone dramatic facelifts. In sport, iconic venues such as the old Wembley Stadium and Highbury, home of Arsenal football club, have fallen by the wayside amid commercial imperatives and the unrelenting drive for progress, replaced by 21st-century, high-tech arenas that many feel lack

LEFT: Children scale a high wall to watch the England vs Australia Ashes Test match at the Oval Cricket Ground, south London, August 1953.

"London is the epitome of our times, and the Rome of today"

Ralph Waldo Emerson

Freedom of the City

The ways in which Londoners choose to spend their leisure time changed dramatically throughout the 20th century. A reduction in average working hours and increased levels of disposable income, along with technological and cultural innovations, have at various times encouraged the city to take on new forms of spectacle and fun.

Entrepreneurs peddling fresh "crazes" have helped ensure a constant stream of new opportunities in the capital. Great leisure barons such as the holiday-camp founder Billy Butlin, the theatre impresario Oswald Stoll and the Odeon cinema creator Oscar Deutsch have all capitalized on the city's appetite for novelty entertainment.

In the first half of the 20th century London's boom in commercialized leisure was exemplified by the rise of cinema. By 1930 the city had 258 registered picture houses, and "going to the flicks" was on its way to overtaking theatre – for centuries a mainstay of London's social and cultural scenes – as the favoured choice for an evening's entertainment.

Indeed, the 1930s were a time of real concern for the world-famous West End theatre industry. The Great Depression combined with a much-opposed Entertainment Tax in the UK took their toll on producers and theatre owners, while the growth of other forms of entertainment, such as cinema and television, added to the concerned rumblings in London's Theatreland.

The cinema boom was most evident around Leicester Square. In 1900 the busy piazza had been lined with opulent Victorian theatres, but by the end of the 1930s, two sides of the square had been given over to glamorous, modern-looking "super-cinemas", whilst the commanding Leicester Square Odeon had taken its place on the site of the old Alhambra music hall.

The pre-war period turned out to be the golden age of London cinema. In the late 1940s, the ubiquitous Odeon chain of art-deco picture houses lost many of its single-screen venues either through closure or conversion into other uses, such as bingo halls.

Other forms of recreation, however, were on the rise. American-style luxury dance halls – called "palais de danse" – attracted Londoners with their offerings of live jazz and swing – two music genres that had crossed the Atlantic from America. The first and most famous of these venues, the Hammersmith Palais, opened in west London in 1919. The Hammersmith Palais would become central to the British music scene, playing a leading role in the introduction of jazz to the UK and showcasing generations of the biggest names in rock and pop. Its lifespan was limited, however, and by the end of the 20th century rising crime in the area, coupled with a refusal by English Heritage to afford it Listed status, had begun its demise. In 2001 the local council allowed it to be demolished and in 2007 property developers brought to an end nine decades of musical history, tearing down the building to replace it with an office block.

Whilst London's bustling nightlife had got into full swing early in the 20th century, Londoners' taste for leisure activities beyond a fun night out took a little longer to materialize. In the first quarter of the century, for the majority of working Londoners, an annual holiday meant a fortnight at the seaside. Then, in 1938, Billy Butlin opened a holiday camp at Clacton in Essex. The Butlins brand was born, and Londoners had a self-contained, multipurpose, family-friendly leisure resort on their doorstep.

Those who couldn't afford a holiday had the option of a trip to a local lido – outdoor swimming areas often located within parks. Throughout much of the 20th century lidos were dotted all over the capital, but in the 1970s most fell into a state of disrepair amid spiralling costs, and only a handful remain today.

Factors such as increased car ownership and the rise of budget airlines continue to entice Londoners beyond the city parameters, but recent years have also seen a surge in popularity of home-based entertainment. In the first half of the 20th century the most popular pastime within the home was listening to the radio, but the proliferation of television channels has slowly eroded its popularity. By far the biggest impact on leisure pursuits, however, particularly amongst the young, has been the rise of new media and the arrival of the Internet.

Today the commercial speculators of 21st-century London must try that bit harder to command the attention of the city's leisure-seekers.

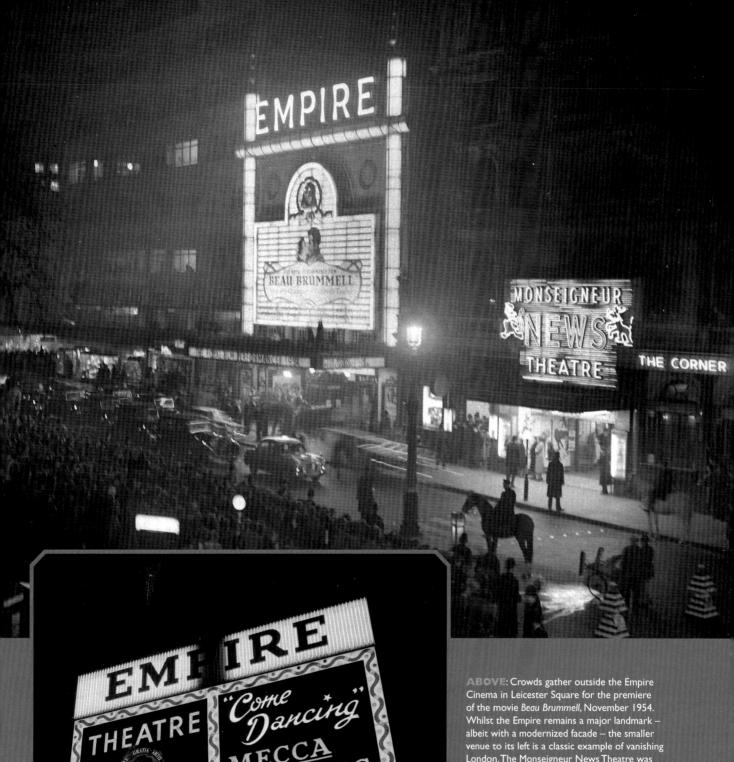

ABOVE: Crowds gather outside the Empire Cinema in Leicester Square for the premiere of the movie *Beau Brummell*, November 1954. Whilst the Empire remains a major landmark – albeit with a modernized facade – the smaller venue to its left is a classic example of vanishing London. The Monseigneur News Theatre was one of several venues of its kind across London and the rest of the UK that offered one-hour news segments to the public. However, with the evolution of television news, the Monseigneur and its counterparts gradually died out.

LEFT: The Empire promotes its latest showings in neon lights, including *It Happened at the*

That's Entertainment

The arrival of theatre on London's cultural landscape came in the early 20th century in the shape of variety theatre (aka vaudeville). Performances took place in large, lavish venues and represented a more refined version of the coarse music hall entertainment that had dominated the previous decades.

However, as the century progressed, London's variety theatres struggled in the face of competition from cinema and television, and by the end of the 1950s many had closed their doors for good. Some, including the Windmill Theatre (pictured right) in Soho, resorted to extreme measures in a bid to draw in punters. The Windmill became famous for its live nude tableaux – a form of visual performance art – but faced renewed competition from the private strip clubs that were popping up across Soho, and finally closed in October 1964.

Cinema, meanwhile, had continued to grow in popularity as the introduction of shorter working hours and higher wages gave Londoners more time and money to spend on leisure pursuits. The effects of this cinematic revolution were felt across the capital, mainly as a result of the efforts of Oscar Deutsch, a scrap-metal merchant from Birmingham who founded the Odeon cinema chain. These new, smaller venues were an ideal fit for the parameters of London suburbia and within years several provincial towns housed one.

With their modern design and decor, cinemas became known as 'dream palaces', offering visitors a glamorous respite from the daily grind of working life. However, during the 1950s, as television became more widely available, cinema declined in popularity. Many of these 'dream palaces' were subsequently demolished or converted into bingo or snooker halls.

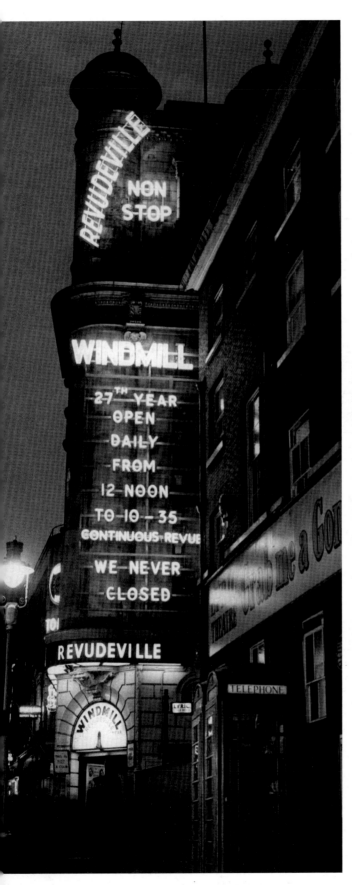

ABOVE: Two female fans standing on a railing at Piccadilly Circus ahead of the premiere of the new Beatles film *Yellow Submarine* at London Pavilion, July 1968. The Pavilion closed its doors as a theatre in 1986, with the interior gutted and converted into a shopping arcade. It is now part of the Trocadero Centre entertainment complex.

OPPOSITE LEFT: The Strand Theatre on Aldwych is lit up at night to advertise the play *Maigret*, November 1965. In 2005, the venue was renamed the Novello Theatre in honour of the Welsh composer and actor Ivor Novello, who lived in a flat above it from 1913 to 1951.

LEFT: The Windmill Theatre on Great Windmill Street, April 1958. The theatre closed in October 1964.

LEFT: The Odeon Cinema in Kingston upon Thames, March 1935.

OPPOSITE: The lavish foyer of the Plaza Cinema, Piccadilly Circus, June 1968. The Plaza was originally a theatre but was converted into a twin cinema in 1967. Further refurbishments in 2004 saw the Plaza all but destroyed with only the outer walls remaining. Now there is a Tesco store on the ground floor, and a new five-screen cinema complex above called Apollo West End.

BELOW: Members of the Living Theatre cast mingling with the audience at the Roundhouse Theatre in Chalk Farm, north London, June 1969. In the 60s and 70s, the Grade II listed Victorian venue, which began life as a railway engine shed, hosted rock gigs by high-profile bands such as The Rolling Stones and Pink Floyd, but later fell into disrepair. In the 1990s the venue enjoyed a resurgence after being refurbished and is now used for performing arts and concerts.

Let's Dance

By the early 1930s London was awash with dance halls. Particularly popular were luxurious, American-style halls known as palais de danse, which offered a swish night out to a backdrop of varying musical styles. The second half of the 20th century saw a fresh wave of London clubs popping up across the capital as new music genres arrived on the cultural scene.

ABOVE: A sign for Gargoyle Club on Meard's Street, March 1965. Founded in 1928, the Gargoyle was a regular haunt for artists, politicians and intellectuals. The popularity of the club began to dwindle in the mid-1950s, and as it fell into decline it became a drinking den – though still prestigious enough to attract high-profile figures such as artists Francis Bacon and Lucian Freud. By the 1970s, a theatre had been added to the top floor, but this could not keep the club afloat. The Gargoyle closed its doors in the late 1970s, and the buildings were listed Grade II in 1978. It is now a hotel and all-day dining room called Dean Street Townhouse.

ABOVE RIGHT: A performance at the Fleet Street Jazz Club, Fetter Lane, December 1954.

RIGHT: The Café Royal on Regent Street, June 1963. The restaurant and meeting place attracted famous patrons throughout the 20th century, but closed in December 2008 to make way for a luxury hotel.

TOP AND LEFT: Dancers at the London Jive Club in Baker Street, November 1956.

ABOVE: Revellers at The Satire Club in the West End perform the "twist" – a new dance craze that had arrived from America, October 1961.

Last Orders

For centuries, London's pubs have been a cornerstone of community life. But like so many of the city's customs and institutions, they have struggled to adapt to modern tastes, lifestyles and economics. Most recently, factors such as the smoking ban, increases in beer duties, cheap supermarket lager, advancements in home entertainment and high operating costs have all contributed to the closure of many of the city's watering holes.

There has also been an important cultural shift; namely, the decline of a male-dominated society. In previous times, it was the thirst of the working man that needed satiating, but now pubs must consider women and children too.

The response has been to make pubs more inclusive. Many of the old city-centre pubs have had their interiors torn out, and replaced with a décor and atmosphere likely to appeal to a younger crowd. Meanwhile, those housed in old bank buildings have been turned into wine and cocktail bars, whilst the proliferation of family-friendly gastropubs has seen restaurant-standard cooking intrude on what was traditionally an informal ambience.

ABOVE: The Cock Tavern on Fleet Street, circa 1935. This distinctively narrow building is an example of London's weakness for preserving its past. The original establishment stood until 1887 when it was replaced by the Law Court's branch of the Bank of England. A replica was built across the road, with many of the original interior furnishings – including the fireplace and mantle – making the short journey too. Unfortunately, a fire in 1990 destroyed many of these original items.

LEFT: Ye Olde Cheshire Cheese pub on Fleet Street, circa 1930. This historical establishment, located in a narrow, unassuming alleyway, is another to survive the pub cull of recent years. It boasts a literary legacy, having been referenced in the Dickens' novel *A Tale of Two Cities*. Indeed, Dickens was said to have been a regular visitor to the pub.

ABOVE: A large concentration of sex shops in Soho, circa 1980. Since the 1980s, streets like this have disappeared as Soho has largely distanced itself from its former reputation as the hub of London's sex industry. Today it is better known as a fashionable district of upmarket restaurants, bars, clubs, shops and media offices.

BELOW LEFT: Punters studying the form guide before placing a bet at William Massey betting shop in Bethnal Green, east London, May 1961.

BELOW RIGHT: Those who thought pay-per-view television was a new concept may be surprised to hear the idea existed way back in the 1960s. Here a family watches a rented, coin-operated television in their London living room, November 1959. Coin-operated TVs worked from a slot meter, with the money collected each week by the company running the service. Rented televisions were an alternative to buying a set in the days when the cost of sets were prohibitively high.

London's Lidos

During the 19th century, public baths were typically used as communal washing facilities, but the arrival of lidos in the 1920s and 30s changed the perception of these shared spaces. Outdoor pools were particularly well-received in an era when sunbathing had become increasingly fashionable and sporting sun-kissed skin was a desirable look.

In their heyday London's lidos were hugely popular – particularly with those who couldn't afford a trip to the seaside – but in the 1960s and 70s many of them fell into disuse due to high maintenance costs. Consequently, only a handful remain across the capital.

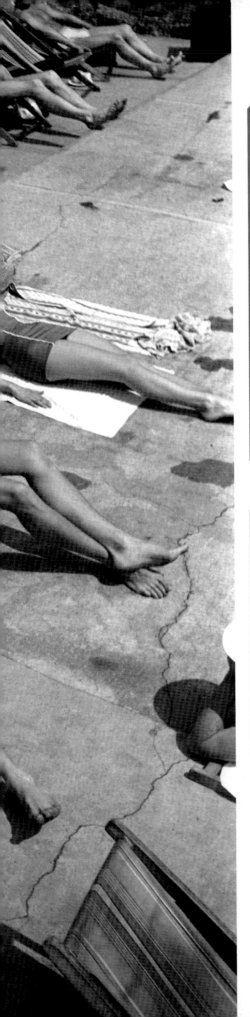

OPPOSITE: Sunbathers at the Oasis Lido in Central London, June 1957.

TOP: A women's beach fashion show is previewed at Ruislip Lido, June 1960. Ruislip Lido was one of London's most popular outdoor swimming venues from the 1930s to the 70s, but declined after the council increased admission prices beyond the reach of many visitors. Numbers dwindled, traders left and the site fell into disrepair. It has now been rebuilt on a smaller scale and is run by volunteers.

ABOVE: Small power boats on the boating lake at Battersea Pleasure Gardens, May 1952. The Pleasure Gardens were created for the Festival of Britain celebrations in 1951 and included a fun fair, restaurants and beer gardens. Much of the site was demolished in the years after the Festival, though a boating lake still remains to this day.

School's Out

The task of comparing the leisure pursuits of children today and those of yesteryear without delving into clichés about games consoles and reality television is a difficult one – yet there is no doubt that life for London's youngsters has changed radically over the years. These photos evoke a time where outdoors represented "freedom". Games such as "conkers" – banned today in some schools due to safety concerns – offered an exciting respite from the authoritarian rigours of lesson-time.

OPPOSITE: Schoolboys playing a game of "conkers", September 1950.

OPPOSITE BELOW: Children at a London comprehensive school leapfrogging over concrete pillars in the playground, April 1965.

BELOW: Inspired by the Wimbledon tennis championships taking place, children enjoy a game of tennis in the back streets around their home in south-east London, July 1961.

RIGHT: Women from the Hampstead Garden Suburbs Institute in north London perform a synchronized exercise during a training routine, circa 1950.

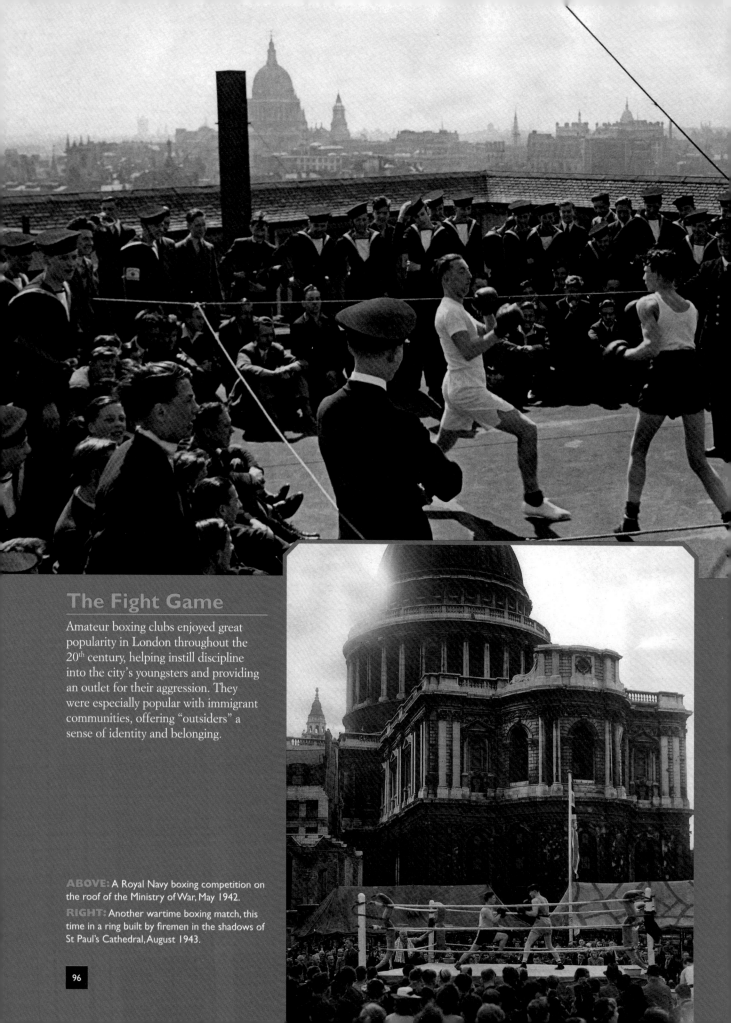

The Fight Game

Amateur boxing clubs enjoyed great popularity in London throughout the 20th century, helping instill discipline into the city's youngsters and providing an outlet for their aggression. They were especially popular with immigrant communities, offering "outsiders" a sense of identity and belonging.

ABOVE: A Royal Navy boxing competition on the roof of the Ministry of War, May 1942.

RIGHT: Another wartime boxing match, this time in a ring built by firemen in the shadows of St Paul's Cathedral, August 1943.

"Even in its sports London had a reputation as a violent city" Peter Ackroyd

Ted 'Kid' Lewis

One fighter to emerge from London's Jewish boxing community was Ted 'Kid' Lewis. Born in the East End as Gershon Mendeloff, he adopted his assumed name whilst a member of the Judean Athletic Club. He had his first fight at 14 and went on to win the World Welterweight Championship and several other British, European, Commonwealth and World titles during his career.

Intriguingly, he is also said to have served as security for fascist politician Oswald Mosley. Legend has it that Lewis brought an abrupt end to his position after questioning Mosley on his anti-Semitic views, and duly striking him in the face.

LEFT AND RIGHT: London-born boxer Henry Cooper takes on Muhammad Ali (then known as Cassius Clay) at Wembley Stadium, June 1963. The photo on the right shows one of the iconic moments in London sporting history, as the legendary Ali lies prostrate after being knocked down by Cooper. However, the bell for the end of the round went just seconds later, depriving Cooper of the chance to finish the job. Ali went on to win the fight. In 1966 they met again, this time at Arsenal Stadium in north London, to contest the world title. Cooper was defeated once more by Ali.

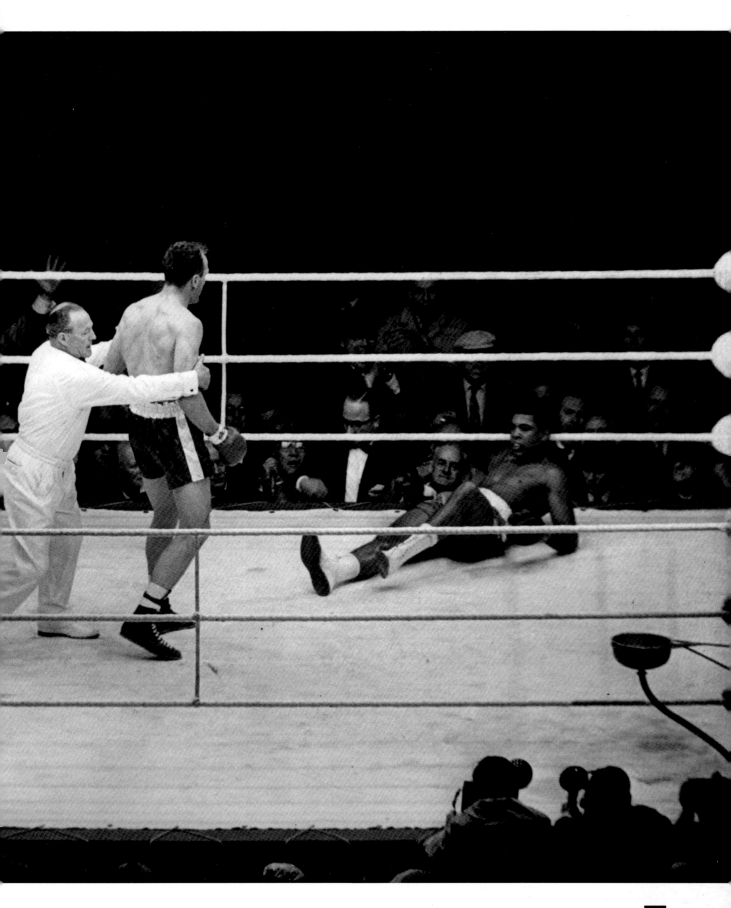

The Glory Game

Football in London has always been unique. No city in Europe has a larger concentration of professional clubs (currently 12) and no city can boast such consistently impressive attendance figures. Even in the lower divisions, thousands flock to watch their teams, week in, week out.

But the game has changed unalterably in the past 20 years. As evidenced by the dressing-room scene on this page, accessibility to players was once a right not a privilege. Photographers could reach the inner sanctums of stadiums and journalists could hold impromptu interviews without the obstacle of a meddling press officer.

And then there are London's lost terraces. In the 1990s, standing areas at major British football grounds were condemned to the past after the Taylor Report into the Hillsborough Disaster – in which 96 Liverpool fans were crushed to death – ruled them to be unsafe. One club, Arsenal, decided to transform their stadium's two terraced areas into state-of-the-art, all-seater stands. However, in 2006 the stadium was demolished (save for two listed facades) and turned into luxury flats, while the club built a new, larger venue down the road to accommodate their growing fan base. It marked the disappearance of one of London's most historic sporting arenas.

ABOVE: Tottenham Hotspur players share baths with each other and the FA Cup trophy at Wembley after defeating Leicester City in the Cup Final, May 1961. The scene offers a stark contrast to the modern footballers' spacious dressing rooms, which are often fitted with luxurious, high-tech facilities such as hydrotherapeutic jacuzzi tubs.

LEFT: London-born footballer Bobby Moore poses for young fans during a West Ham United training session, August 1962. Moore had made his England debut just a few months earlier. Four years later he captained his country to World Cup glory against West Germany at Wembley Stadium.

OPPOSITE INSET: He may look like a homeless person, but this gentleman is in fact a dedicated football fan ensuring he is first in line for a ticket to the FA Cup semi-final replay between Arsenal and Chelsea, March 1950. In the days before the Internet and ticketing phone lines, fans would often have to queue up at unearthly hours to secure their presence at significant games.

OPPOSITE RIGHT: A view from the terraces at Arsenal Stadium (aka Highbury), north London, March 1981.

London
Zeitgeist

At the turn of the 20th century, London's fashion and cultural scenes were kept in check by a prevailing societal conservatism. The city's sartorial trailblazers were its aristocrats, and culture came from high society alone. This milieu of inhibition lasted until the 1920s, when fashion aligned itself with youth for the first time. It proved a powerful coalition that transformed the cultural landscape of London.

From the charleston dancers of the 20s through to the punks of the 70s, each group has had their moment in the limelight before making way for the next bright thing. Their legacies continue to burn thanks to the popularity of retro style and a broad appetite for nostalgia, but a sense of loss endures, felt most acutely by those who lived amongst them.

"London refuses nobody" Peter Ackroyd

ABOVE: Teenage skinheads performing the moonstomp, a dance derived from music genres including reggae, ska and dub, 1980.

Bright Young Things

London's status as a cultural and fashion capital dates back centuries. But whereas at one time the role models and influencers were establishment figures from royalty and the aristocratic elite, the 20th-century trailblazers were the city's youths.

Home to one of the largest working-class populations in Europe, London has been a fertile breeding ground for the kind of disaffectedness and rebellion from which new fashions and subcultures so often emerge. Moreover, the size of the capital has the capacity to accommodate diversity, which in turn has created an atmosphere of rivalry and one-upmanship, as characterized, for instance, by the hostilities between the Mods and Rockers in the 60s, and an enduring – though ostensibly friendly – tribalism between the city's north, south, east and west territories.

Pivotal in drawing such divergent groups together was the transport revolution of the early 20th century, which brought the city's vibrant West End district within reach of everyone. With the increased mobility came a renewed appetite to develop the city into an entertainments hub, and nightlife venues began popping up across the capital.

In the 1920s a seminal figure emerged who would weld together fashion and culture in London. Norman Hartnell was a successful costume designer who grew to greater prominence once he began designing for the consumer market. His formal yet playful and colourful dresses sat well with the hedonistic mood of London's young aristocrats, and within a decade he was accepting design orders from the Royal Family, his name established across the globe.

Hartnell was still designing in the 1960s, and his influence is considered by many to have helped London challenge Paris' supremacy as the fashion centre of the world. But it would be an altogether different spirit and style that would come to define that particular decade; one that revolted against everything Hartnell and the hitherto conservative British couture industry represented.

If the 1960s did not quite begin in a wild fashion frenzy, it certainly ended with one. The first half of the decade saw the city clinging doggedly to the more conservative 50s styles. Fashions started to change with the revealing and controversial miniskirt – created by the London-born designer Mary Quant – and the accompanying A-line dress designs of the mid-60s, which served as an ideal vehicle for the psychedelic styles that were becoming popular in the boutiques that lined London's colourful Carnaby Street in Soho.

At the same time, with unemployment virtually non-existent as compared to today, the city's plethora of post-war baby boomers found themselves enjoying a surfeit of disposable income. The items on which they chose to spend most of it were pop music and clothes.

Some of the most prolific spenders were the Teddy boys – London's original teen rebels – who had helped erode the stigma of men "dressing to impress" with their stylish, dandy-inspired apparel. Now both sexes were increasingly fashion-conscious and the trend-makers had a new and captive audience – the youth market. The Teddy boys were the first of London's new wave of subcultures to emerge in the second half of the 20th century, when music and fashion served as cultural mobilizers, offering the city's youths the inspiration to forge original identities.

In the 1970s, the fashion designer Vivienne Westwood also marked a new mood in London, yet drew her inspiration from a darker set of references to the kaleidoscopic hedonism of the previous decade. Instead her clothes resonated with echoes from London's anti-establishment and disaffected youth cults, from Teddy boys to punk rockers.

Fashion's alliance with youth also proved a powerful force in revamping the cultural topography of London in the 1970s, with dowdy, rundown neighbourhoods transformed into vibrant, trendy areas. Camden Town in north London was a notable recipient of this change, acquiring a newfound reputation for bohemian, alternative culture. But the most dramatic development took place in west London, in Notting Hill Gate, where Afro-Caribbean immigrants helped to spark a localized cultural revolution, transforming the area from notoriously poor and deprived to pulsating and hip over the course of just 15 years.

In the last quarter of the 20th century one of the starkest cultural transitions took place in the east London district of Shoreditch and neighbouring Hoxton. Formerly a predominantly working-class area, it has been gentrified by the creative industries of art, design, advertising, fashion and music. Today it is a haven for artists and fashionistas, who congregate in a ramshackle area of narrow streets and converted warehouses, all the while contributing to a new spirit of the age.

ABOVE: Punk band the Sex Pistols, circa 1976. The band emerged from the King's Road, west London, in the early 1970s and helped initiate the punk movement in the United Kingdom.

The Bowler Hat

Prior to the 1960s, London fashion was characterized by conservatism and conformism – and nothing epitomized this sartorial tone more than the bowler hat, designed in the 1850s and named after hat-makers Thomas and William Bowler. It was immediately popular as a less formal alternative to the top hat, which was traditionally associated with the upper classes. Bowlers soon became a British cultural icon and were famously worn by the comedians Charlie Chaplin and Laurel and Hardy. They also became a key element in the look of London's traditionally-dressed city workforce, along with pinstripe suits, briefcases and umbrellas.

ABOVE: Male members of the Royal Family, including the Prince of Wales (later King Edward VIII) and Prince Albert (King George VI) at the Stock Exchange in London, circa 1925.

OPPOSITE: A dapper gentleman wearing a bowler hat on the streets of London, circa 1950s.

LEFT: Women in traditional Edwardian clothing take a stroll in Hyde Park, circa 1905.

The Swinging Sixties

The 1960s was an era that divided London into "before" and "after". Quite simply, the entire cultural atmosphere was transformed, as the city took on a new identity as an exuberant centre of youth culture. In 1966 the American magazine *Time* printed a cover story which dubbed London "the swinging city", depicting it as a place of freedom and self-expression, and at the vanguard of popular culture. London would never be the same again.

OPPOSITE: Models in mini dresses pose in front of a decorated London bus, circa 1960s. The miniskirt, created by British fashion designer Mary Quant, became synonymous with London's Swinging Sixties.

BELOW: The Apple Boutique, on the corner of Baker Street and Paddington Street, still wrapped in scaffolding three days before its opening, December 1967. The shop, which mainly sold fashion garments and accessories, was a short-lived business venture launched by pop band The Beatles. It lasted less than seven months before closing. The building was demolished in 1974 and is now used as office space.

OPPOSITE: A music fan sports a "hippy" look at a Rolling Stones concert in Hyde Park, July 1969. More than 300,000 fans attended the concert held in memory of guitarist Brian Jones, who had died two days earlier.

RIGHT: Fashion designer Vivienne Westwood at the Swatch shop in Oxford Street with her newly released watch The Orb, circa 1960s. Having moved to London as a teenager, Westwood helped shape the city's fashion landscape throughout the 1960s, '70s and '80s, most notably bringing modern punk and new-wave fashions into the mainstream. It was her contribution, along with a troupe of cultural change-makers, which turned London into the fashion capital, not just of Britain, but of the world.

Dedicated Followers of Fashion

At the heart of London's Swinging Sixties was Carnaby Street in Soho. A shop called "His Clothes", owned by John Stephen – an influential fashion designer who ended up owning several stores on the street – became a Mecca for London's "mod" followers, and before long the entire street was brimming with trendy outlets bringing new fashions to the masses.

However, Carnaby Street's time as a fashion centre was limited. In the 1980s, as the counterculture punk movement swept across Britain, the street began losing its appeal. Many young people stopped conforming to trends and fashions, and instead rebelled against them. The street's decline continued until the late 1990s, when a property company injected new life back into the area. These days Carnaby Street is a veritable tourist attraction, and retains vestiges of its former glory through retro stores that evoke the spirit of the 60s.

LEFT AND ABOVE: Trendy boutiques in Carnaby Street, circa 1960s. "Paul's" menswear store is of particular significance to your author, whose father worked there in the midst of 60s London.

OPPOSITE: "Mod" fashion in Carnaby Street, October 1966.

Pearly Kings and Queens

Fashion is characteristically transitory, but try telling that to London's Pearly Kings and Queens. Their apparel has barely changed since the late 19th century, when this unique band of champions of the working class emerged from groups of "costermongers" – street vendors for fruit and vegetables. They would become a permanent symbol of the city, representing London's penchant for ritualism, provenance and eccentricity.

As London expanded its geographical boundaries, costermongers in each borough elected a "Coster King" to fight for their rights – almost an early form of trade unionism. Lampooning the wealthy West End society who would often wear pearls on their clothes, the kings and their wives would sew lines of pearls onto their own hand-me-downs.

This evolved into the elaborate costume we know today when a road sweeper called Henry Croft completely smothered a worn-out dress suit and top hat with pearl buttons. Croft was a strong advocate of the costers' outlook on life – to help those less well off, even if you had little yourself – and incorporated the slogan "All For Charity" into his attire.

The outfits delighted onlookers and worked wonders in raising funds for the various charities supported by the costers. Before long, all of the kings and queens from London's 28 boroughs produced their own Pearly costumes.

Today around 30 Pearly families continue to serve in various London districts where they maintain their long tradition of charity fund-raising.

LEFT: Pearly Kings and Queens celebrate Covent Garden's 300th birthday, May 1970.

Teddy Boy Style

With their quaffed hair, drape jac[...]
and narrow 'drainpipe' trousers, [...]
London's Teddy boys were the firs[...]
face of post-war British youth cult[...]
Inspired by Edwardian dandies, th[...]
emerged in the 1950s and went on[...]
infiltrate literature, music and cine[...]

The British pop boom of the 1960[...]
fully embraced by the Teddy boys –[...]
notably the rock and roll music tha[...]
been exported from America. Som[...]
Teddy boys gained notoriety follow[...]
violent clashes with rival gangs. The[...]
most notable was the 1958 Notting[...]
riots, in which they were implicated[...]
attacks on the West Indian commun[...]

During the 1970s, a new generation[...]
Teddy boys emerged. Their inimitab[...]
look had been refined to include lou[...]
colours inspired by glam rock. This [...]
wave was bolstered by fashion design[...]
Vivienne Westwood and her boyfrien[...]
Malcolm McLaren (later the Sex Pist[...]
band manager) through their shop "L[...]
it Rock" on the King's Road in Chels[...]
which sold typical Teddy boy attire.

As with most subcultures, the Teddy
boys only had a limited shelf life,
though the early 1990s saw a revival
by a group known as The Edwardian
Drape Society (T.E.D.S), based in the
Tottenham area of north London.

RIGHT: Teddy boys, 1956.

BELOW: Teddy boy Tony Reuter leader of
the Elephant Boys gang seen here showing
off his knife, 1955.

ABOVE: Teddy boys on the King's Road in Chelsea, west London, circa 1976.

LEFT: Mods and Rockers clash at a pop concert, 1970.

Mods and Rockers

During the early 1960s, two gang subcultures surfaced in London, leading to a moral panic in the British media over their violent exchanges. The Mods, with their clean-cut appearance and stylish scooters, were in stark contrast to the Rockers with their black leather jackets and powerful motorbikes.

But the divide went beyond the aesthetic; it was also a clash of personalities. Rockers considered Mods to be effeminate and snobbish, whilst Mods thought Rockers were behind the times, dirty and uncouth.

Their battle ground was often outside of London – in holiday towns such as Margate, Brighton, Hastings and Southend, where the gangs would converge for organized fights. The clashes were invariably reported by the media in a sensationalized manner, sparking national concerns about the country's dysfunctional youth.

By the end of the decade, however, the Mods and Rockers had faded from public view. Media attention had instead turned to emerging youth subcultures, including hippies, skinheads and punks.

Rockers (opposite) and Hell's Angels, one up from Rockers (above).

RIGHT: London Mods show off their scooters, May 1964.

Sound City

London's contribution to the music world has been immense. From vaudeville to music halls, pleasure gardens to symphony orchestras, the city has been at the cutting edge of music for centuries. Throughout the 20th century London consistently produced some of the world's most highly regarded musicians. The 1960s in particular were a prolific decade for nascent bands emerging from every corner of the city. It was also the decade in which the rock and roll phenomenon that had taken the world by storm arrived in London.

OPPOSITE: Punk rock band The Clash, circa 1977. The band, which formed in London in the mid-1970s, wrote one of the most famous songs about the city, 'London Calling', which appeared on the album of the same name.

LEFT: The Rolling Stones at the Royal Albert Hall in 1963. Their manager put them in matching outfits – it didn't last!

BELOW: The Who at Charlton's ground – The Valley – in 1976. Formed in West London in the mid 1960s, their music is often described as being the soundtrack to an era. The band was particularly popular with the "Mods" subculture of the 1960s and 70s.

Breaking London

Not only does London produce world class musicians – it also attracts them. Just as the holy grail for UK musicians is to "break" America, making your name on the London music scene as an outsider also comes with a certain cachet. As a consequence almost every major musician and band from outside the city has at one point or another come to London, including The Beatles, who during their reign as the Kings of Pop in the 1960s, used Abbey Road Studios in St John's Wood, north-west London, to produce most of their albums.

ABOVE: Musician Jimi Hendrix at his Mayfair flat in London, January 1969. The American guitarist and singer-songwriter lived in the upper floors of 23 Brook Street between 1968 and 1969. In September 1970, London was also the scene of Hendrix's death, after he overdosed on sleeping pills at his girlfriend's flat in Notting Hill, west London.

OPPOSITE: American musician Bob Dylan walking past a shop window in Central London, May 1966. Dylan had made his first trip to London four years earlier, performing at several of the city's folk clubs, including Les Cousins, The Pinder of Wakefield and Bunjies.

Punk Culture

Punks first emerged in London in the mid-1970s as an anarchic and aggressive movement whose visual identity, music and politics reflected their rebellious doctrine. Its followers were counterculturalists who not only distanced themselves from mainstream society, but opposed the very ideologies behind it. A focal point of the punk look was the hair which was spiked as high as possible into a Mohican style.

ABOVE: A teenage punk girl with distinctive spiky hair, April 1983.

OPPOSITE: Punk devotees at Sloane Square, west London, on the first anniversary of the death of Sex Pistols' guitarist Sid Vicious, February 1980. One fan sports a leather jacket with the anti-Semitic message "Belsen was a gas" on the back, a reference to the notorious German concentration camp from the Second World War.

RIGHT: A punk sitting amongst broken plastic beer glasses at the 10th anniversary of the last Sex Pistols concert at the 100 Club on Oxford Street, January 1988. In 2010, it was announced that the legendary 100 Club would close at the end of the year owing to continuing losses. However, a campaign was launched to keep the venue open, supported by musicians including Paul McCartney, and it survived the threat of closure.

Celluloid City

For non-natives, their perception of London is defined largely by its portrayal in popular culture. One of the most photographed cities in the world has also been rendered on celluloid as much as any other except New York. And just as the comedies of Woody Allen have served to romanticize the Big Apple, films set in London have also helped to define the urban vernacular of the city. From Hitchcock's thrillers to the Ealing Comedies of the 1940s and 50s, through to the crime dramas starring that most inimitable of Londoners, Michael Caine (pictured opposite), London's movies have informed our understanding of the city.

OPPOSITE: American actress Raquel Welch draws attention outside a pub in Fulham, west London, during a break in filming for the movie *Bedazzled*, circa 1967.

LEFT: London-born actor Michael Caine, July 1964.

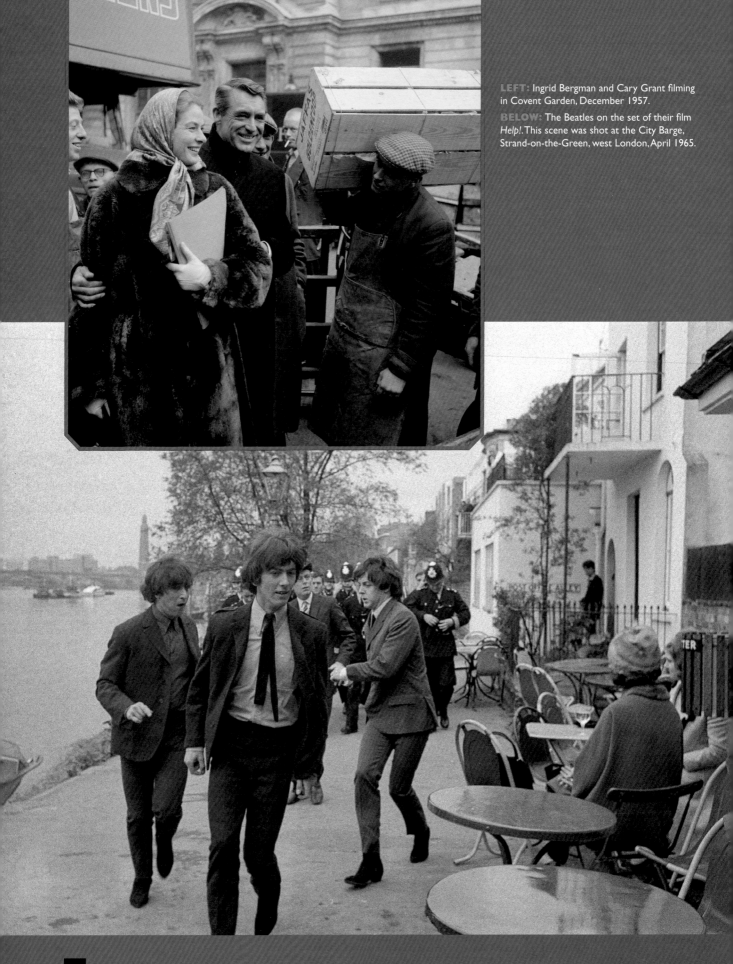

LEFT: Ingrid Bergman and Cary Grant filming in Covent Garden, December 1957.

BELOW: The Beatles on the set of their film *Help!*. This scene was shot at the City Barge, Strand-on-the-Green, west London, April 1965.

ABOVE: Eric Sykes on location at Victoria station for the movie *Village of Daughters*, October 1961.

LEFT: A short break in filming *The Magic Christian* for Peter Sellers and Ringo Starr – both competent photographers.

Kinetic London

No feature of London has undergone a more prolific transformation than its transport. Whilst the city's streets retain many of their former characteristics, the vehicles that traverse them are incomparable to a century ago. The driving force for progress – as is so often the case – has been technology. Advancements over the years have resulted in the phasing out of several types of vehicle in favour of more efficient models, often requiring less human endeavour. In some cases, such as the London tram, the entire mode of transport has been abandoned.

One constant throughout the 20th century has been the iconic London Underground. The rapid transit system was built in the mid-19th century in response to the city's burgeoning population and the advent of the suburban commuter. Whilst the majority of the original network has remained, there are several disused – or "ghost" stations that have garnered interest amongst Tube enthusiasts over the years, some of which can be spotted whilst passing through the modern-day system.

"By seeing London, I have seen as much of life as the world can show"

Samuel Johnson

From Horse Play to Road Rage

Transport has been a major contributor in defining the shape of London. Whatever the prevailing architectural style, the single most important element in changing the look and feel of the capital's cityscape has been the myriad vehicles that have traversed its roads and rails.

By far the most influential vehicle has been the motor car. In 1900 horse-drawn vehicles and pedestrians created traffic congestion. By the end of the century, London's roads were dominated by cars – two million, no less – along with an assortment of paraphernalia such as traffic lights, yellow lines, parking meters and zebra crossings, all of which served to transform the appearance of the city.

However, the advent of the private car and the independence it offered was not without its problems. After first appearing on the streets of London in the 1890s, worries about reckless driving soon followed. The various forms of traffic on London's roads – motorized, horse-drawn and bicycles – was a potent and often lethal combination, and in 1906 the first case of manslaughter caused by driving was tried at the Old Bailey.

In the early years of the 20th century, technology provided the impetus for a transport revolution in London. The first electric trams went into service in 1901 and within 15 years they had rendered horse trams surplus to requirements. The transfer of buses from horse-driven to mechanized was an even quicker process, once petrol engines had proved their reliability.

The survival of horse-drawn cabs lasted a little longer – as did any goods vehicles that were reliant on horses. Indeed, horse-drawn milk carts could still be seen on the streets of London well into the 1950s.

As well as reshaping London's roads, new technology was also changing its rail networks. Improved tunnelling methods, reliable safety lifts and non-polluting electric power were all vital in enabling deep-level Tube construction. London's first Underground line opened in 1890, and within two decades a vast subterranean network had given the city another dimension in its pursuit of rapid and efficient transit of its citizens.

The improvement in public transport served to create a more mobile city. The Tube network took the strain off the roads above, making bus and tram journeys both faster and cheaper. Commuting some distance to work by public transport, and leisure travel at weekends, were now viable options, and the idea of living in the suburbs no longer meant an entire change in lifestyle. Indeed, the development of London's transport network was a major factor in the rapid growth of outer London in the 1920s and 1930s, while the population of the inner city declined.

By the 1930s London was enjoying a golden age of improvements to its transport infrastructure, which was now respected across the world. Trams were being replaced by trolleybuses, while petrol was making way for diesel as a more efficient means of powering London's growing fleet of vehicles.

The outbreak of the Second World War brought an abrupt end to the programme of improvements the city's transport had enjoyed since the turn of the century. In the years since, London's transport system has seemed to limp through a series of problems and crises revolving around how it can be funded and managed in a sustainable way.

Of all the changes, perhaps the most high-profile casualty has been London's Routemaster bus. Since its introduction in 1956 the red double-decker bus had become an iconic piece of London's street furniture, but by the end of the century it was considered to be polluting, unwieldy and impractical for modern use. It was officially withdrawn from public service in 2005.

Despite a century of road widening and traffic-control measures, the city ended the 20th century with substantial traffic congestion and frustrating parking restrictions. By the 1990s the average traffic speed in Central London during rush hour was 10mph – not that different to the horse-drawn transport at the beginning of the century. Amid great controversy, a congestion charge was implemented to ease the burden. The motor car, for so long emblematic of a flourishing capital city, by the end of the 20th century became, in the eyes of many, a symbol of encumbrance and unsustainability.

ABOVE: A see-through motor car using experimental glass is trialled in Central London, April 1968.

LEFT: A city gent grips his bowler on a two-wheeled taxi, circa 1960s. The female driver worked for a London firm that hoped to start a moped taxi service.

RIGHT: A double-decker bus with a fuel trailer attached, March 1943.

BELOW: A pensioner on a self-made lying down bicycle equipped with floats as he makes his first voyage on the River Thames at Laleham, Greater London, May 1972.

Horses for Courses

In the first quarter of the 19th century, public transport in London was prohibitively expensive to the vast majority of its citizens. It was not until the Parisian-influenced arrival of horse-drawn transport in the late 1920s that Londoners were able to traverse the city quickly, efficiently and at affordable prices.

For the remainder of the century, the horse-drawn bus remained largely unchanged, with the potential for modification curbed by the limited load that a pair of horses could pull. One way of increasing the number of passengers that could be carried was to run the vehicle on rails set into the road. By pulling a carriage on steel rails, friction was reduced, making it much easier for a pair of horses to haul a heavier weight.

In 1870, following a decade of fine-tuning, London's first horse-drawn tram service began. Being able to carry more passengers than a bus whilst using the same number of horses meant that fares could be dropped. This brought public transport within reach of many more working people and enabled them to live further out from their workplaces in the crowded city centre.

But for all of its benefits, horse-drawn transport was ultimately an uneconomical system. Fifty thousand horses were required to keep London moving, with each animal needing to be fed, watered, stabled and groomed. In the latter part of the 19th century, operators looked for an alternative to the horse that would be both cheaper and more efficient. The electrification of the trams and the arrival of the motor bus in London just before the First World War led to the gradual demise of the working horse on London's streets.

OPPOSITE: Horse-drawn buses carrying passengers in Piccadilly, 1904.

BELOW: Drivers from The Old Cab Drivers' Association navigate horse-drawn hackney cabs around Lincoln Inns Field as part of a test to show they are still capable of handling the vehicles, May 1921.

ABOVE: An omnibus heading for Oxford Street, September 1909.

OPPOSITE: A female passenger enters a London taxi cab, June 1933. Before the arrival of motorized vehicles, taxis in London were in the form of horse-drawn "Hackney Carriages". By the 1920s, motorized taxis were a common sight on London's streets.

Traffic Control

There was a time when much of London's traffic was controlled, not by traffic lights or other electronic means but by the London Bobby who kept things moving... most of the time.

The Tram comes to London

As construction of the Underground train system continued apace, 1861 saw the introduction of a new system of transport on street level – the tramway. It was introduced by the appropriately named George Francis Train, who hailed from America where the tram was already well established. The first London route opened in March 1861, between Marble Arch and Notting Hill.

The vehicles were drawn by a pair of horses and could accommodate over 30 passengers. With metal wheels running on smooth tracks in the road, they were much easier to pull than their hackney carriage predecessors, which ran on uneven road surfaces.

However, there were several objections. Taxi drivers saw them as a potential threat to their own overcrowded market whilst the rumbling of the steel wheels on the rails created substantial noise pollution. Another problem was that the rails jutted above the road surface, causing a serious hazard to other vehicles. The experiment was abandoned by the authorities.

At the end of the decade the concept was revisited and parliament authorized three tramlines in London – but all running outside the city centre to avert complaints about noise levels. The horse-drawn trams ran uninterrupted for 30 years, but changes were on the way. In April 1901, the first electric trams appeared in London, drawing power from overhead electrified wires. Large numbers of passengers used the new trams, which were widely seen as being glamorous, modern, efficient and clean.

By 1924 more Londoners were travelling by tram than by any other form of transport. But competition was never far away. In the 1930s motor buses began to appear on the streets, offering a more flexible level of service and greater comfort. Then, in 1931 the trolleybus – a cross between trams and buses – was introduced.

Throughout the 1920s and 30s trams increasingly came to be seen as noisy and dangerous to other road users and by the early 1930s the golden age of the tram was drawing to a close. Following a failed push to modernize the system, a Royal Commission in 1931 recommended that trams be replaced by trolleybuses. The process got under way in earnest in 1935 and by 1940 more than half of London's trams had been scrapped.

The programme was interrupted during the Second World War but plans to resume it were announced in 1946. The final London trams ran in 1952, and were honoured with a week-long farewell celebration. The final tram ran from Woolwich to New Cross on 5 July.

SPECIAL

1988

The Rise and Fall of the Trolleybus

Trolleybuses, which drew electricity from connected overhead wires, replaced trams in London in the mid-20th century. However, the era of the trolleybus was brief. The need for expansion of routes into the growing suburbs, cheap oil fuels and the cost of maintaining overhead wires made them inefficient and unviable. London's last trolleybus ran in May 1962. Their replacement came in the shape of the iconic Routemaster bus, but the transition took some getting used to for the drivers, many of whom stayed on to operate the new form of transport. Each driver was required to pass a diesel bus driving test before taking to the wheel of the new models.

ABOVE: London's last trolleybus journey is made in the presence of vast crowds, gathered to mark the sentimental event, May 1962.

OPPOSITE: A trolleybus making its way through Finchley, north London, circa 1955.

The Legendary Routemaster

To casual observers, the iconic red London bus may appear alive and well. But the reality is that over the past 35 years, a much cherished incarnation of the famous vehicle has suffered a steady and terminal decline.

The Routemaster bus was developed between 1947 and 1956, offering unique features including an open platform which allowed boarding and alighting away from stops, and the presence of a conductor enabling minimal boarding time and optimal security.

For over a decade they proliferated and became part of the London street furniture. However, the late 1960s saw a transition towards buses operated solely by the driver, and production of Routemasters was halted. The existing Routemaster fleet remained largely intact for around 15 years, but in the early 1980s a gradual withdrawal of the vehicles began.

During the new millennium, debates surrounded the issue of whether to replace or retain the Routemaster. Supporters cited its speed of boarding and tourist appeal, while opponents pointed to the economics of running increasingly elderly buses when more advanced designs were now on the market.

In 2004, Mayor of London Ken Livingstone announced the phasing out of the Routemaster in favour of a new bus service fully accessible to wheelchair users. The Routemaster was officially withdrawn from general service in December 2005, although it remains in regular service on two "heritage" routes.

LEFT: Tourists sit underneath umbrellas on the top deck of an open-top bus during a sightseeing tour of London, October 1976.

OPPOSITE: A London Transport Routemaster bus at the Chiswick garage with a crew of a driver, conductor and ticket inspector.

Unsung Heroes

Up until the early 1980s, conductors, or "clippies", were a common feature of many bus services in London. The necessity for conductors was due to the layout of the vehicles, which separated the driver from the passenger saloon by allowing entry at the rear. The conductor would communicate with the driver using a series of bell codes, such as two bells to start. They were vital to the smooth running of the city's bus system.

The double-decked Routemaster bus was developed between 1947 and 1956, offering unique features including an open platform for boarding and alighting away from designated stops, and the presence of a conductor.

For over a decade they proliferated and became an easily recognizable part of London's street furniture. However, the late 1960s saw a transition towards buses operated solely by the driver, and the production of Routemasters was halted. The existing Routemaster fleet remained largely intact for around 15 years, but in the early 1980s a gradual withdrawal of the vehicles began.

OPPOSITE ABOVE: A conductor looks out from the platform of his Routemaster bus during one of London's "pea-souper" smog outbreaks, December 1962.

OPPOSITE BELOW: A female bus conductor taking a fare, September 1919. The following month, all of London's women conductors lost their jobs as they were replaced by men returning from the First World War.

LEFT: A member of the Chiswick Accident Demonstration Unit of the London Transport Executive shows a bus conductor how accidents are caused by throwing himself off the bus, December 1950.

The Age of Steam

Images of trains letting off steam at London's grand old stations are laced with evocative potency. The age of steam in fact predates the railways and can be traced back to the Industrial Revolution.

Then, at the beginning of the 19th century, a little-known engineer called Richard Trevithick pioneered a steam engine capable of powering the large-scale transportation of cargo. Steam trains including the Flying Scotsman and Golden Arrow (pictured right and on the following page, respectively), which would begin their routes in London, became much-valued means of transport.

Steam engines remained the dominant source of power well into the 20th century, when advances in the design of electric motors and internal combustion engines resulted in the vast majority being replaced by more sophisticated and efficient alternatives.

LEFT: The Flying Scotsman steam train leaving King's Cross station on its first ever non-stop run to Scotland, May 1928. The express train has been running between London and the Scottish capital Edinburgh since the mid-19th century, and in 1934 became the first steam locomotive to clear 100mph. In the 1950s, steam versions of the train were replaced by diesel.

RIGHT: Light streaming through the lattice roof of Euston station, as a steam locomotive pulls away from the platform, 1928.

BELOW: The Golden Arrow train sitting at London Victoria station, April 1946. The luxury boat train linked London with the port of Dover on the south coast of England, where passengers would pick up ferries to mainland Europe. Market forces, including the increased popularity of air travel, saw a decline in demand for the Golden Arrow, and the service ran for the last time in September 1972.

OPPOSITE: Journey's end for London commuters at Liverpool Street station during the 1950s.

LEFT: The Short S.45 Solent 2 flying boat on the River Thames during celebrations of 30 years of British civil air transport, May 1949.

London's Original Airport

The town of Croydon in south London was once home to one of the world's most important transport hubs. Between the World Wars, Croydon Airport became synonymous with the glamour and romance of air travel. For those who couldn't afford leisure trips, the airport was still a popular attraction, with visitors coming to watch aircrafts landing and taking off – or, for just a few shillings, enjoy a short flight over London.

During the Second World War, the airport was used as an RAF fighter station. By the time it was returned to civilian control, technological advancements had led to the creation of larger aircrafts. Croydon was too small to accommodate the new fleet, and its end was nigh. The last scheduled plane left its tarmac in September 1959.

ABOVE: A Fokker Princess Xenia landing at Croydon Airport, 1928.

ABOVE RIGHT: An Air France Bloch 220 aircraft pictured at Croydon.

RIGHT: The Arsenal football team and officials about to board an Imperial Airways flight to Paris, October 1932.

City in
Ruins

Throughout its history London has periodically been a wounded city. The damage inflicted by the two World Wars of the 20th century left physical scars that are still visible today, including shrapnel marks and bullet holes on edifice walls. Much of the city was simply destroyed, with the most intense period of bombing razing more than one-third of London's buildings in a matter of days.

Yet London has not only suffered at the hands of international aggressors; it has endured domestic violence too. Politically motivated demonstrations, such as the Miners' Strike of 1984, have often degenerated into riots, while sporadic racial tension has also resulted in bloody violence on London's streets.

"*London is like some huge prehistoric animal, capable of enduring terrible injuries, mangled and bleeding from many wounds, and yet preserving its life and movement*" Winston Churchill

ABOVE: Smoke rises from behind the dome of St Paul's Cathedral after the first daylight bombing raid, 1940.

Damage Limitation

When London has come under attack from war or terrorism it has often left tangible scars that have permanently changed the city. More subtle has been the emotional impact that war and terrorism have had on its people.

When the first German bombs fell on London in 1915, a year after the start of the First World War, it was the first time in two centuries that the city had come under direct attack. By the time the war had ended the capital's death toll was 600. In comparison with what would follow in the not-too-distant years to come, the physical damage to the city was limited – but the era of the explosive air-borne bomb offered a new threat to unsettle the psyche of every Londoner.

In 1940, a year after the start of the Second World War, the Nazis unleashed a wave of attacks on London that came to be known as the Blitz – after the German word "Blitzkrieg", meaning "Lightning War". For 11 weeks the capital was bombed virtually every night, creating a massive firestorm and a death toll that ran to more than 20,000.

By the end of the Blitz, parts of Central and east London had been razed to the ground. A third of the capital's housing stock was destroyed or damaged, and thousands of Londoners were left mourning the loss of family and friends.

The landscape of ruin left by the bombing attacks changed the city forever, but war would also have more far-reaching societal consequences, not least amongst London's workforce. As discussed in Chapter 2, men going away to war meant that women were drawn into the workplace in larger numbers than ever before. It marked the moment when the idea of gender equality in modern Britain entered the mainstream.

In the same vein, life for the city's lower classes would also be irrevocably changed. After the war, the renewed sense of comradeship amongst citizens encouraged amendments in social reform. Before long, equal standards of health and education for all, irrespective of class or background, had been implemented.

More controversial was the growing presence of the state in Londoners' daily lives. Food rationing, identity cards, licensing laws, censorship, wage freezes, price ceilings, curfews and other restrictions were all a product of wartime conditions.

Identity cards were the most contentious development. First introduced in 1915 to help military conscription and food rationing, they were made compulsory in 1918, with citizens required to carry their cards and produce them on demand. The system came to an end in 1919 but was revived in 1939. Identity cards lasted through to the end of food rationing in 1952, but the idea survived and the end of the 20th century saw the government lobbying for their reintroduction.

Whilst peacetime after the end of the First World War marked a watershed moment in geopolitics, domestic harmony in Britain did not last. The 1922 creation of the Irish Free State had left the six Northern Ireland counties of Ulster under British colonial rule and ushered in 80 years of bitter skirmishes between the British and the IRA (Irish Republican Army). The battle was taken intermittently to the streets of London by IRA bombing campaigns, which were at their most intense during the 1970s.

Compared to the two World Wars, the damage inflicted on the city by the IRA was limited to compact areas. But the threat of terrorist attacks affected the city's appearance in ways both big and small. In the 1980s, after a spate of IRA bombings, dustbins in which explosive devices could be planted were removed from the streets.

Then in 1993, to counter the IRA's use of vehicles packed with explosives, the city began implementing a series of security measures called the "Ring of Steel" – a 6.4-mile unbroken security cordon encircling London's financial heart, comprising various obstructions including bollards and police boxes.

The ring, which stretches from Aldgate to the Strand, and from Shoreditch to the Temple, also includes CCTV and other equipment that allows police to monitor and record every car that enters the City. London was hit again in July 2005, this time by Muslim extremists who detonated four bombs on the city's transport network. The ring – the most radical shift to the urban order of any part of London in decades – continues to evolve, shaping who uses the city, and for what purpose.

London has carried the burden of its physical and emotional wounds into the 21st century. Wartime bombs left a legacy of empty spaces where buildings had once stood; the ruins of 17th-century churches were preserved as reminders of the trauma. The psychological effects remain immeasurable, but are forever connected to the city in the enduring evocation of the "Blitz spirit".

ABOVE: A view from the dome of St Paul's Cathedral as it burns during the Second Great Fire of London, December 1940.

LEFT: Firemen fighting a blaze next to St Paul's Cathedral, December 1940.

168

The War to End all Wars

To modern-day peaceniks, the enthusiasm for war in 1914 would have been shocking. Rallies were frequently held in Trafalgar Square where armbands were issued to men who promised to enlist, and white feathers – representing cowardice – to those who refused. Thousands of soldiers marched through the capital to attract recruits, carrying a banner inscribed with the words "Wake up, London!"

As it transpired, London was not awakened by bombing until May 1915, but, by the end of the conflict, almost every family in the capital had been affected by the death or wounding of a relative or friend. Of more than 1 million London men who enlisted in the army, 131,000 died on active service. Armistice was signed on 11 November 1918, although peace was not officially declared until 28 June 1919, when thousands flocked onto the streets of London to celebrate.

OPPOSITE: Men queue to join the army at Scotland Yard in Central London at the start of the First World War, August 1914. Around 80,000 London men were already serving in Britain's armed forces. Encouraged by propaganda and nationalist fervour, many more eagerly joined the ranks.

ABOVE RIGHT: Women queue to buy war bonds at Trafalgar Square, October 1917. Civilians were encouraged to "do their bit" by purchasing war bonds and savings certificates to help finance the war effort.

MIDDLE: A mob attacks a German-owned tobacconist and a newsagent in Poplar, east London, following the sinking of the British ocean liner *Lusitania* by a German U-boat, May 1915. The war devastated London's vast German community, with all Germans in the capital registered as "alien enemies", and those of military age held in internment camps. The Olympia Exhibition Hall in west London and Alexandra Palace became makeshift prisons, holding as many as 3,000 German detainees.

RIGHT: A poorly attended anti-conscription meeting in Hyde Park illustrates the public's enduring appetite for war, December 1916. Britain's first conscription law had been passed 10 months earlier after it became clear that the war would drag on far longer than anticipated. In later years, conscription became known as "National Service", until the law was abolished in 1960.

The Second World War

In September 1938, an iconic moment in 20th-century British politics took place at the inconspicuous setting of Heston Airport in Hounslow, Greater London. Standing on the tarmac surrounded by officials and media, Prime Minister Neville Chamberlain held aloft a piece of paper signed by himself and German Chancellor Adolf Hitler.

The paper was headed "The Anglo-German Agreement" and included a statement that the two nations shared a desire to "never go to war again". Chamberlain had just returned from Munich where the ill-fated "Munich Agreement" had been signed by the Germans and other European powers. From the airport, Chamberlain travelled to Downing Street where he delivered his famous "Peace for Our Time" speech, in which he confidently predicted that conflict had been averted. Less than a year later, Britain was at war with Germany.

OPPOSITE: Prime Minister Neville Chamberlain at Heston Airport in Hounslow, Greater London, holding the agreement that he claimed would end the imminent threat of the Second World War, 30 September 1938.

TOP: East End residents dig a trench for a communal air raid shelter in their back gardens on the day Hitler and Nazi Germany invaded Poland, 1 September 1939.

ABOVE LEFT: An East End family leaving the city with their belongings on the back of a horse and cart, September 1940.

ABOVE RIGHT: Firemen reading their newspapers outside their sandbagged fire station at Kensington Close, west London, during the Blitz.

> *"London has always been energetic and powerful enough to buttress itself against distress and disaster"* Peter Ackroyd

The Blitz

In July 1940, thousands of German planes were sent across the English Channel to attack British airbases. The offensive triggered the "Battle of Britain", which proved victorious for the defending nation. In August 1940, a change of strategy saw German bombers begin targeting British cities, including Manchester, Coventry and London. The new attacks were designed to destroy public morale by targeting civilian as well as industrial and military landmarks.

For 11 dark weeks, London endured uninterrupted night time bombings in the period known as the Blitz. Over a third of the city was destroyed, including most of the London Docks, while some 17 of Christopher Wren's churches were badly damaged. The casualty toll was huge: more than 20,000 dead and over 50,000 badly injured.

London carried the scars of the Blitz into the 21st century. A legacy of empty spaces were left where buildings had once stood, whilst the ruins of damaged churches were preserved as gloomy reminders of the ordeal.

ABOVE: Repairs underway on the Charing Cross Road where a bomb had created a large crater, November 1940.

OPPOSITE: A scene of destruction in Central London after air raids had taken their toll, circa 1941.

ABOVE: A burnt-out building on Cannon Street with St Paul's Cathedral still standing firm in the background, circa 1940. St Paul's famously endured numerous close calls during Second World War air raids. Indeed, it was struck by bombs in both October 1940 and April 1941, but both times only superficial damage was inflicted. In September 1940 a time-delayed bomb that had struck the cathedral was successfully defused and removed by the Royal Engineers, under the command of Lieutenant Robert Davies. Had this bomb detonated, it would have destroyed the cathedral. As a result of this action, Davies was awarded the George Cross, along with Combat Engineer George Cameron Wylie.

"London has always been a vast ocean in which survival is not certain" Peter Ackroyd

BELOW: A double-decker bus after being thrown against the side of a house by a bomb blast during a Second World War air raid, September 1940.

Subterranean Sanctuary

During the First World War, the authorities adopted a "blind eye" policy to the large numbers of people who sought shelter in London Underground stations. As the Second World War began, the official line became that of discouragement, for fear of Londoners developing a "deep shelter mentality" and refusing to return to the surface.

The new guidelines were in vain, and the image of people sheltering in the Underground network became synonymous with London during the war. The government even backed down sufficiently to begin providing toilets, bedding and food to those underground, and later constructed deep-level bunkers under several stations, capable of holding some 8,000 people.

Some stations were also used to protect treasured national artifacts. In 1917, the disused platform at Aldwych station in Westminster was used as storage for 300 pictures from the National Gallery. During the Second World War, the tunnels between Aldwych and Holborn were used to keep items from the British Museum, including the classical Greek sculptures, the Elgin Marbles.

But more than providing a safe haven, stations also helped the city to function as normal throughout the war. Defying frequent disruptions and a huge shortage of train staff, hundreds of thousands of Londoners continued travelling to their destinations on the Underground every day.

RIGHT: Londoners sleep on the tracks at Aldwych Underground station during the Second World War. Having started life as Strand in 1907 (its name changed to Aldwych in 1915) the station was perpetually threatened with closure due to low passenger numbers. After operating only during peak hours for more than 30 years, Aldwych finally closed in 1993 and is now one of London's historic disused stations.

ABOVE: A teacher gives children a maths lesson in the Elephant and Castle Underground station as they shelter during an air raid alert, March 1941.

RIGHT: Nurses give shelterers medicine for the prevention of flu as they take cover in St Johns Wood Underground station, 1941.

ABOVE: A woman adjusts her top bunk as she prepares for a night's sleep in an air raid shelter, 1940.

LEFT: Families take cover underground.

Keeping London Moving

Above ground, London's transport system and its staff played an important part in keeping the city moving during the Second World War – and often in the most perilous of conditions. During blackouts, buses ran with reduced lighting and drivers could barely see beyond a couple of metres ahead of them, whilst the vehicle's windows were covered with anti-blast netting to stop them shattering in the event of a bomb explosion.

LEFT: A London bus alongside St Paul's churchyard during a night-time air raid, December 1940.

Internal Damage

Most images from the Blitz show the panoramic devastation caused by the bombing raids, but less documented is the damage inflicted in isolation. In one night alone, the City of London lost a third of its floor space. The resulting blaze, which became known as the Second Great Fire of London, could be seen 30 miles away, with the flames leaping the river and igniting a line of warehouses on the south bank. Paternoster Row, an ancient street and the centre of London's book trade since the 18th century, was entirely obliterated. More than 6 million books went up in flames. In place of the street today is Paternoster Square.

At the prestigious nightspot Café de Paris in Piccadilly, two German landmines fell through the roof straight onto the dance floor. Eighty people were killed, including jazz dancer Ken "Snakehips" Johnston who was performing onstage at the time. At the start of the war the Café had been allowed to stay open even though other venues were closed by order. The venue's maître d', Martin Poulson, had convinced the authorities that the building's four solid storeys of masonry were sufficient protection against air raids.

ABOVE AND RIGHT:
A bombshell is removed from
Brixton Hill, south London.

OPPOSITE ABOVE: A
salvage worker sorts through
damaged band instruments at
the Café de Paris in Piccadilly,
March 1941.

OPPOSITE BELOW:
Lambeth Palace Library in
south London after being
bombed, circa 1941.

LEFT: The damaged interior
of the Guildhall in the City of
London, December 1940.

The Prefab

The Prefabricated home was a necessity after the extensive damage inflicted on London during the Blitz. While they were initially seen as temporary dwellings, they lasted for far longer than had been anticipated, with the last big Prefab estate being demolished only recently.

The Troubles come to London

London's status as a major capital city has also seen it embroiled in conflicts of international power. The overseas dispute that most affected the city in the 20th century took place in Ireland, with the efforts of the six Northern Irish counties of Ulster to extricate themselves from British colonial rule. Their battle was taken to the streets of London by the Provisional IRA, who launched bombing campaigns that were at their most intense during the 1970s. There were 36 bombs alone in London in 1973.

The IRA's aim was to shake the resolve of the public and put pressure on the British government to concede to their political demands. Their campaign was aided by London's large Irish community in which IRA active service units were able to move easily.

A ceasefire was reached in July 1997, but the peace was short-lived. In 2000, the Real IRA, an Irish republican splinter group, began a new series of attacks on London. In July 2005, the IRA's Army Council announced an end to its armed campaign. The IRA decommissioned its arms between July and September 2005.

OPPOSITE AND ABOVE: The aftermath of an IRA bomb blast outside Scotland Yard Metropolitan Police headquarters on Victoria Embankment, Westminster, March 1973. On the same day, another bomb exploded outside the Old Bailey courts, while two more were defused in other areas of the city. One person died and almost 200 were injured in the two explosions.

ABOVE: Damage to the GPO Tower (aka the BT Tower) in Central London, showing shattered windows and a missing wall after an IRA bomb blast, November 1971.

OPPOSITE FAR LEFT: The scene after an IRA bombing of the Baltic Exchange in the City of London, April 1992.

OPPOSITE ABOVE: An IRA bomb explodes in Bishopsgate in the City of London, clouding the NatWest Tower in smoke and debris, April 1993.

OPPOSITE LEFT: The Bishopsgate bomb leaves a chasm in a parade of buildings where the Church of St Ethelburga had stood.

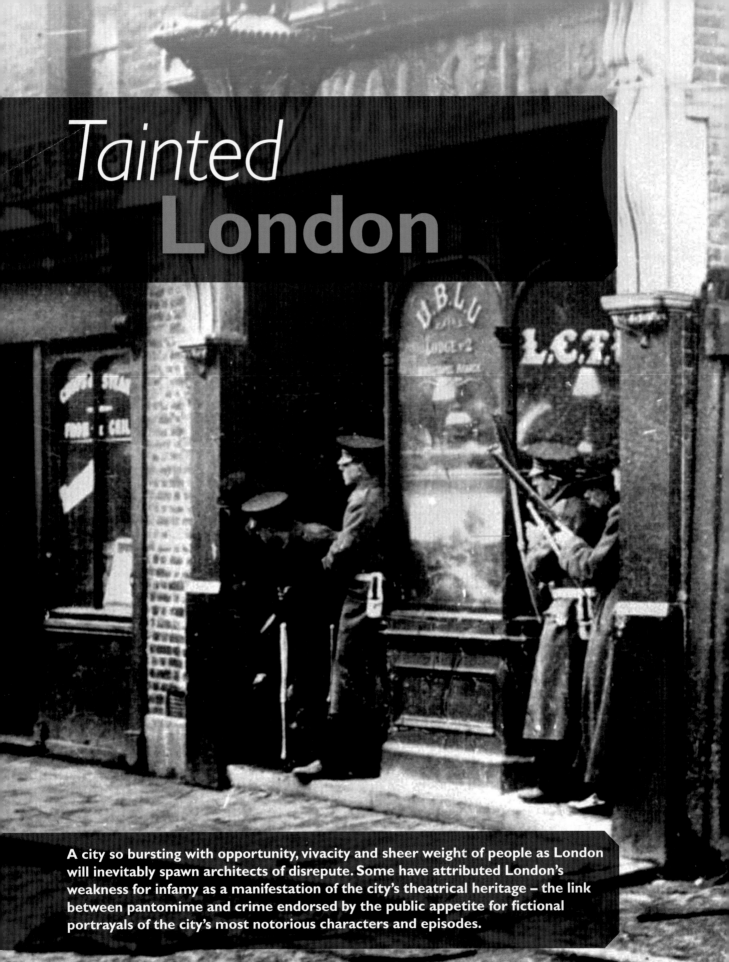

Tainted
London

A city so bursting with opportunity, vivacity and sheer weight of people as London will inevitably spawn architects of disrepute. Some have attributed London's weakness for infamy as a manifestation of the city's theatrical heritage – the link between pantomime and crime endorsed by the public appetite for fictional portrayals of the city's most notorious characters and episodes.

"*In London mythology, the greatest heroes are often the greatest criminals*" Peter Ackroyd

ABOVE: Police officers consider their options during the Siege of Sidney Street, January 1911. At the front of the officers, wearing a bowler hat, is Winston Churchill, who was home secretary at the time and had been called to the scene to assess the situation.

Murder, Mayhem and Mischief

London's rough edges have never been fully ironed out. The city has persistently acted as a magnet and breeding ground for shadowy characters, whose misdemeanours have, on occasion, forced the city into a state of introspection.

The major change in the 20th century as far as criminality is concerned was the ways in which the perpetrators and their motives were perceived and understood. Until the 1900s, criminal behaviour in Britain was most often equated with individuals of the lower social classes, whose transgressions were seen to be symptomatic of a lack of moral fibre. By the turn of the 20th century, however, developments in psychiatry had led to many criminals being identified as suffering from some form of behavioural abnormality that had been either inherited or nurtured by dissolute and feckless parents. All such perceptions informed the way that criminals were treated by the criminal justice system, and before long Victorian liberal ideas began to feed into penal policy.

Perhaps the most tangible example of how this shift affected London was the demolition of the city's notorious Newgate Prison, which remained in use for more than 700 years, and has featured in a number of novels and films about British history. The prison's squalid conditions inspired many social reformers to campaign for its closure, and when it was eventually destroyed in 1902 it symbolized the new and enlightened attitudes towards crime, morality and retribution that had been ushered in with the new century.

In the 1722 novel *Moll Flanders*, the author Daniel Defoe described Newgate as "an emblem of hell itself". It was the kind of hyperbole that would have appealed to the burgeoning tabloid newspaper industry of the early 20th century, which saw crime as an easy vehicle on which to spread moral panic and boost readership figures. For instance, the murders perpetrated by the ill-famed serial killer Jack the Ripper in the autumn of 1888 were confined to a small area of London's East End, yet provoked a nationwide panic whipped up by press sensationalism. The media had realized that violence, especially violence with a sexual frisson, fed the public's appetite for salacious news.

Whilst Londoners have often responded to crime with the basest of instincts (as shown in the Ripper case), they have also shown a willingness to take a more considered view. Throughout the 20th century, London was the scene of a large number of high-profile crimes, some of which would spark debates about the wider issue of how to tackle criminality.

In 1953, special constable John Christie was hung for killing at least six women – including his wife and daughter – at his flat at Rillington Place in Notting Hill, west London. Two years later, nightclub hostess Ruth Ellis was hanged for the murder of her lover, David Blakely in Hampstead, north London. Both of these cases provoked such intense national interest – even being discussed in government – that they are widely considered to have contributed to the eventual abolition of capital punishment for murder in the United Kingdom in 1965.

Whilst these crimes were followed with an often morbid fascination, they did not capture the imagination in the same way as the criminal gangs that have periodically emerged in London throughout the 20th century. The most notorious of these gangs was controlled by the Kray brothers in the 1960s, but decades before, London was plagued by mob warfare as vicious and terrifying as anything that would follow. Across the city, territorial tribes fought pitched battles for honour and pride: the Bethnal Green Boys hunted Hackney's Broadway Boys, Clerkenwell fought Somers Town, the Red Hands took on Deptford and the Silver Hatchets terrorized Islington. These criminal mobsters would often retain a veneer of respectability through ostensibly legitimate business interests whilst ruling demarcated areas of the city – aka "turfs" – through fear and fascination, ably assisted by loyal henchmen.

Whilst gangs remain one of London's biggest social problems, advancements in policing methods, stricter business regulations and a more interventionist media have made it improbable that a single group could achieve such fame and notoriety in the capital as the Krays and their contemporaries.

London is still capable of harbouring a violent and transgressive underbelly, but, for the most part, it is reined in by the city's progressive instincts. The sheer size of the capital has also ensured that disorder, when it occurs, never threatens to overwhelm the city. It is perhaps the mark of its greatness that London can carry the weight of its imperfections with insouciant but knowing dignity.

ABOVE AND RIGHT: Two of London's most notorious gangsters from the mid-20th century. Pictured right is Billy Hill, December 1954. Pictured above is Jack "Spot" Comer, circa 1950s. During the 50s the pair formed an alliance and referred to themselves as "the Kings of the Underworld". However, they later fell out, with Spot winning the influential support of the Kray twins in the aftermath of the dispute. Nevertheless, in May 1956, Spot was ambushed outside his apartment in Bayswater, west London, by two young thugs, Frankie Fraser and Alf Warren. The incident signalled the end of an era. Jack Spot departed the gangster scene and bought a furniture store, while Billy Hill also "retired" and moved to a villa in southern Spain.

London's House of Death

Between Holburn Circus and St Paul's Cathedral today stands the Central Criminal Court, also known as the Old Bailey. But until the turn of the 21st century a very different institution of justice was located here.

Newgate Prison was for centuries the largest and most notorious of London's jails. In 1780 it was the scene of a massive uprising as part of the Gordon riots – an anti-Catholic revolt that saw rioting take place across London. The prison was set on fire, many prisoners died during the blaze, and hundreds escaped to temporary freedom.

In the late 18th century executions were moved from the public gallows at Tyburn – where Marble Arch now stands – to Newgate. Public burnings and hangings were initially carried out in the prison's open area, and every week large crowds would assemble and pay to watch the executions, lending an element of theatre to proceedings. However in 1868 public executions were abolished and moved to the comparatively private environs of Newgate's inner walls.

Newgate was demolished in 1902, along with the Central Criminal Court next door. Building began on the site in 1903 – using as much of the prison stone as possible – and three years later the Old Bailey was finished. Newgate's gallows were moved to Pentonville Prison in Islington, along with its male prisoners. The female prisoners were transferred to Holloway Prison for women, also in Islington.

ABOVE: Stocks used to restrain prisoners at the notorious prison.

OPPOSITE: Guards at an entrance to Newgate Prison.

LEFT: A gloomy-looking prison walkway at Newgate.

BELOW: Cells and staircases at Newgate Prison.

"An emblem of hell itself" Daniel Defoe

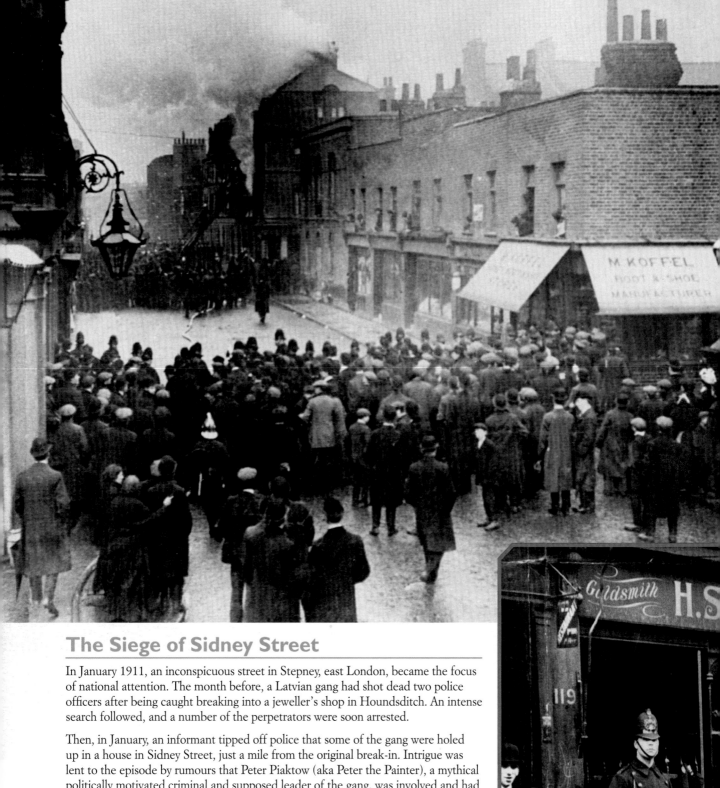

The Siege of Sidney Street

In January 1911, an inconspicuous street in Stepney, east London, became the focus of national attention. The month before, a Latvian gang had shot dead two police officers after being caught breaking into a jeweller's shop in Houndsditch. An intense search followed, and a number of the perpetrators were soon arrested.

Then, in January, an informant tipped off police that some of the gang were holed up in a house in Sidney Street, just a mile from the original break-in. Intrigue was lent to the episode by rumours that Peter Piaktow (aka Peter the Painter), a mythical politically motivated criminal and supposed leader of the gang, was involved and had also taken refuge in the house.

Two hundred police officers were summoned to the scene and they swiftly cordoned off the area. The Tower of London was called for backup, and word got to Home Secretary Winston Churchill, who arrived on the spot to observe the incident first hand and offer advice.

After a six-hour stand-off, a fire began to consume the building. The police stood ready, guns aimed at the front door, waiting for the men inside to attempt their escape. The door never opened. Inside, the remains of two members of the gang were recovered. Peter the Painter was not one of them, and his legend lives on to this day.

ABOVE: Police officers checking their weapons at the scene.

OPPOSITE: Crowds gather on Sidney Street during the siege.

LEFT: Police outside the jewellery shop that the Latvian gang had broken into before their escape to Sidney Street.

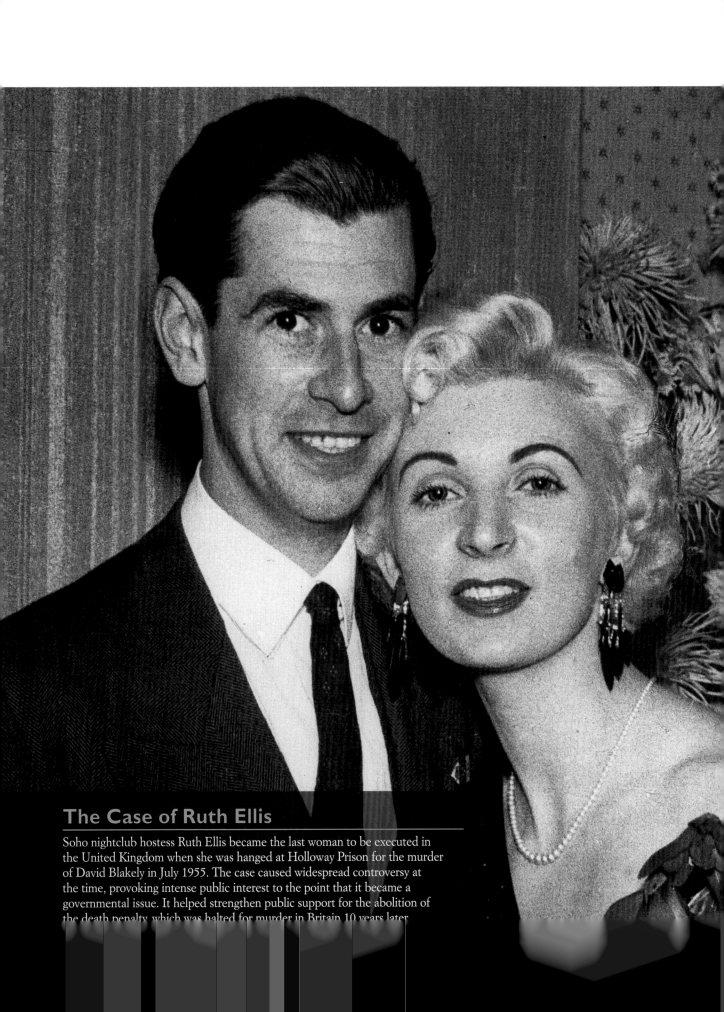

The Case of Ruth Ellis

Soho nightclub hostess Ruth Ellis became the last woman to be executed in the United Kingdom when she was hanged at Holloway Prison for the murder of David Blakely in July 1955. The case caused widespread controversy at the time, provoking intense public interest to the point that it became a governmental issue. It helped strengthen public support for the abolition of the death penalty, which was halted for murder in Britain 10 years later.

'Capital Punishment
Amendment Act, 1868'

The sentence of the law passed
upon Ruth Ellis
found guilty of murder, will be
carried into execution at 9 a.m.
to-morrow.

ABOVE: Crowds gather outside the entrance to Holloway Prison on the day of Ruth Ellis' execution.

OPPOSITE: Ruth Ellis and boyfriend David Blakely, circa 1950s.

RIGHT: A notice of the hanging of Ruth Ellis on a prison door on the day of her execution.

LEFT: A mass of people attend a British Union of Fascists meeting in Hyde Park, September 1934.

Radical London

As the country's political and cultural heartland, London has always been a focal point for national campaigns and protests. Many of the rights and freedoms enjoyed in the United Kingdom today are a result of those who have descended on the city to fight perceived injustice. But whilst rebellion has consistently been played out on London's streets over the years, the themes of dissent have changed dramatically. Social and economic progress has eroded many of the inequalities suffered by previous generations – but it was London's forebearers who sowed those first seeds of change.

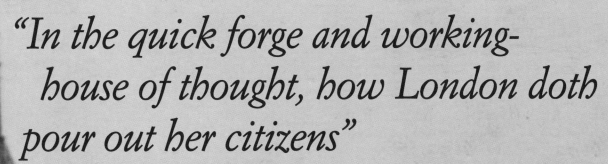

"In the quick forge and working-house of thought, how London doth pour out her citizens"

William Shakespeare

ABOVE: Suffragettes on a boat at Putney Bridge with notices announcing an upcoming Votes For Women demonstration in Hyde Park, 1908.

Rebels with a Cause

London has a rich history of subversion and revolt. During the 20th century the city was at the epicentre of the nation's efforts to battle inequality, prejudice and perceived social injustice.

As the 20th century began, Londoners were living in what had become the political and financial capital of the world. Yet despite the overriding atmosphere of prosperity, some of the worst excesses of the Victorian era – including child labour – remained a blight on society. The golden age, however, had not blinded Londoners to the widespread disenfranchisement that still lingered across the city and beyond, and a prevailing spirit of enlightenment would soon draw its citizens on to the streets to confront national issues of contention.

In the years approaching the First World War, the big battle taking place was for the emancipation of women and, most pressingly, their fight for political franchise. The Suffragette Movement had migrated from northern England to London, where it hoped to raise its profile and gain popular support. Today, sufficient strides have been made in the cause of gender equality to have removed the need for an organized, militant and sustained campaign such as that waged by this valiant band of women.

Between the two World Wars, a major cause of national concern was the rise of the fascist movement. In 1936 an assortment of dissenters – including Jews, communists and socialists – led a huge anti-fascist parade against Oswald Mosley's Blackshirts who had descended on London's East End to propagate their prejudices. The Battle of Cable Street is considered by many to be a significant turning point in the demise of Britain's fascists as a credible political group. By the end of the 1930s the prevailing threat of fascism came from overseas, as Nazi Germany unleashed its warped ideologies on Europe.

Throughout the Second World War, London was a city united, but on occasion there was reason for militant action. With Londoners left to face bombing without adequate protection, a major source of controversy was the government's reluctance to open up deep Tube stations as air-raid shelters. Eventually the will of the people forced the government to back-track and permit Londoners to retreat underground to escape the menaces above.

After the war ended, ordinary folk once again took action, this time to tackle the huge housing shortage caused by the bombing of vast swathes of the city's dwellings. In response, a squatting movement emerged who made it their business to find homes for London's new dispossessed.

The reactions of Londoners to war have always been instructive of the time. In 1900 popular support for the British war against the Boers (Dutch settlers) in South Africa ran high, as thousands gathered in Trafalgar Square to cheer what was seen as a glorious adventure. Similarly, less than a decade later, the First World War was ushered in with unabashed enthusiasm across the city. However, London's appetite for conflict was eroded by the advent of the nuclear bomb and its accompanying horrors, as well as by the emergence of mass media, which allowed the terrors of war to be played out on television in people's homes. Since the 1950s huge anti-war demos have taken place in London, including in 1968 when thousands gathered outside the American Embassy in Grosvenor Square to protest against the long-running conflict in Vietnam.

The fight for workers' rights has also achieved varying degrees of success throughout the 20th century. In the 1930s unemployed miners and shipbuilders marched from the north of England to London to raise awareness of their plight, whilst Poll Tax demonstrations in the 1990s continued the tradition of organized protests taking place on London's streets. Trafalgar Square, in particular, played a role throughout the century as the nation's most important space for political protest.

Every battle fought by Londoners throughout the 20th century is, to some extent, on-going. Women have won the vote but continue to fight for absolute gender equality, racial tension fluctuates amid the sensitive issue of immigration, and the power of the trade unions – eroded by Margaret Thatcher's Conservative government – endures to the extent that labour strikes are still able to cause major disruption across the country.

As London surges into the 21st century, the city can expect to be the intermittent staging ground for those leading the way in the continued pursuit of a postmodern greater good.

ABOVE: Members of the Gay Liberation Front dressed in drag are arrested at the Festival of Light in Hyde Park, September 1971. The men were using the event – organized by an evangelical Christian movement promoting "traditional family values" – to further the cause of gay rights.

The Suffragettes

The women who formed and campaigned for the Suffragette Movement – one of the most influential political groups of the 20th century – are part of the lost iconography of London. The fight for gender equality continues to this day, but the trailblazers were a remarkable band of women – and thousands who supported them – whose formal, elegant appearance belied an unyielding resolve to overturn oppression at all costs.

At the turn of the century women had been campaigning for the right to vote in UK parliamentary elections for over 50 years. But it was not until the creation of the Women's Social and Political Union in 1903 that the struggle gained real momentum. Founded in Manchester by Emmeline Pankhurst, the Union vowed to put "direct action" at the forefront of their efforts.

At the same time London's role as a staging ground for protest was growing. The UK media was becoming increasingly London-centric and the Union realized that to gain maximum attention, it required a base in the capital.

In 1904 the Suffragette Movement transferred its crusade from Manchester to London. For the next eight years, their struggle became highly public and often violent. A faction of the Union advocated hard-line action, including attacking police officers and committing arson. There was a certain incongruousness about images of these primly dressed women participating in militant activities.

The move to the political hub of the country also enabled the suffragettes to maintain a constant presence in Whitehall, where they would heckle members of parliament and chain themselves to government buildings. Several spectacular demonstrations were held, including Women's Sunday in June 1908, which saw suffragettes from all over the UK march through Central London.

In 1918 women over 30 were given the right to vote, and 10 years later women over 21 (the same age men were allowed to vote at the time) were also afforded the same privilege. Another milestone came in 1919 when Nancy Astor became the first woman to enter the House of Commons as an elected member of parliament. Political feminism had achieved a major victory and delivered the impetus for further social and cultural reform throughout the century.

RIGHT: Christabel Pankhurst, daughter of Emmeline, addresses a meeting of the unemployed in Trafalgar Square, 1908.

BELOW: Remnants of the tea pavilion at Kew Gardens after an arson attack by two women connected to the suffragettes, 1913.

VOTE
FOR
WOME
WE DEMAND
THE
VOTE
THIS
SESSION!
WOMENS SOCIA
AND
ITICAL UNION
VOTES
FOR
OMEN
E DEMAND
THE
VOTE
THIS
SESSION!
SOCIAL &
UNION.

United Colours

The lack of colour photography from the period means that the significance of the suffragettes' distinctive apparel is lost on many. Like political parties, the suffragettes adopted colours to represent their mission. They used three, each symbolizing an aspect of the movement. Purple represented freedom and dignity, white stood for purity and green for hope.

The suffragettes' mantra was also evident in the jewellery they wore. Gold, white metal and violet were used because the initials of the three elements – G, W and V – stood for "Give Women Votes". This code enabled any woman wearing the jewellery to be instantly recognized as a supporter of the movement.

ABOVE: Emmeline Pankhurst is escorted by police after her arrest in London, circa 1910. Pankhurst was arrested seven times whilst leader of the Suffragette Movement.

LEFT: A Suffragettes demonstration, May 1906.

Sentiments of Retribution

The ways in which the criminal and iniquitous segments of London society have been perceived over the years has changed radically. Certainly we have come a long way since Victorian times when the notion of a "criminal class", and that of a "crime gene" passed down through generations, were widely accepted.

Up until the 1960s questions about how to deal with extreme criminality invariably revolved around the subject of capital punishment. The last executions in the UK took place in 1964, but the death penalty actually remained on the statute book for certain other offences – including treason and espionage – until the 1990s.

In general, debates about capital punishment were confined to parliament and dinner-party discussion. It was only when individual cases captured the public's interest that people were drawn onto the streets to protest for their respective standpoint.

London, of course, was the stage for several such protests. The city's Holloway, Pentonville and Wandsworth prisons were all used for the execution of prisoners, including such infamous figures as William Joyce (the last person to be hung for treason in the UK) and Ruth Ellis.

OPPOSITE: Members of the public carry placards demonstrating against the execution of Ronald Marwood at Pentonville Prison, north London, 1959. Marwood, who had been found guilty of stabbing a police officer to death during a street fight, was hanged in May that year.

OPPOSITE BELOW: The gallows at London's notorious Newgate Prison before it was demolished to build the Central Criminal Court (the Old Bailey) in 1904.

RIGHT: A notice board for the execution of William Joyce, aka Lord Haw Haw, outside Wandsworth Prison in south-west London, on the eve of his execution for treason, January 1946. Joyce was found guilty of broadcasting Nazi propaganda to the United Kingdom via radio transmissions from Germany during the Second World War.

BELOW: Eric Wildman, president of the National Society for the Retention of Corporal Punishment, with propaganda boards petitioning against the abolition of corporal punishment on a London street, November 1947. It was officially abolished across the United Kingdom the following year.

1926 The General Strike

In May 1926 an event took place that proved to be a watershed for labour relations in the United Kingdom. Following years of industrial disputes within the coal industry, miners in the North of England, Scotland and Wales opted to strike in protest against an enforced pay cut.

Meanwhile in London, printers in Fleet Street – then the home of the British press – were refusing to print an article for the *Daily Mail* newspaper that criticized trade unions. In response, the Trades Union Congress (TUC) made a call for all union members in essential industries to join the miners' strike action.

From 3 May, some 2 million workers across the country went on strike. In London, dockers, printers, power station workers, railwaymen and transport workers all joined the picket line. The government responded by bringing in the army to ensure that essential services continued and food supplies got through. It was an unnerving sight to witness armoured vehicles on the streets of London during peacetime.

The decision of the capital's print workers to down tools caused a vacuum in news dissemination. Winston Churchill, chancellor of the exchequer at the time and famously opposed to strike action, convinced the government to publish its own newspaper in order to get its view across to the nation. For eight of the 10 strike days, the *British Gazette* newspaper was printed in Paris and flown to London.

On 13 May, after a series of fruitless negotiations with the government, the TUC called an end to the strike. Many strikers refused to return to work in protest against the TUC climbdown, and stayed on the picket line for another six days.

The disruption caused by the strike was enough to convince the government that such scenes could never be repeated. A year later, a new Trade Disputes Act was passed that effectively outlawed the sympathetic strike action that had brought London, and the nation, to a standstill.

TOP: Armoured cars on London streets during the General Strike, May 1926.

ABOVE: Buses driven by volunteers seen here in Oxford Street, during the 10th day of the General Strike.

LEFT: Special constables receive their helmets during the General Strike.

BELOW LEFT: Soldiers seen here patrolling the streets in and around the City of London driving their Austin armoured cars, on the 8th day of the General Strike.

BELOW: A temporary milk depot is set up in Hyde Park. The park was used for army barracks during the Strike.

1984 The Miners' Strike

Some political and social struggles lie dormant, others bubble away under a fragile surface, while a few remain won or lost forever. One longstanding cause that is almost certain to never rise again is that of the nation's coal miners.

The mining industry is one of Britain's great lost industries, having been all but wiped out over the course of the 20th century. Much of its terminal decline was played out on London's streets, not least in 1984 when miners descended from the North – the industry's traditional heartland – in protest against mass pit closures. What followed proved to be the final confrontation between the country's workers and the state.

Just as the suffragettes had uprooted to London 80 years earlier, the nation's unemployed coal miners marched from the north to the capital to raise awareness of their plight. Their cause was led by Arthur Scargill, president of the National Union of Mineworkers (NUM), who had been instrumental in organizing the 1973 Miners' Strike that ultimately sounded the death knell for Edward Heath's Conservative government.

This time his direct opponent was Prime Minister Margaret Thatcher, whose determination to diminish the power and influence of the unions characterized her period in office – and defined her legacy.

The strike lasted for nearly a year and ended in defeat for the miners. They returned to work on 5 March 1985. Politically, in the minds of many, it was the day that the Right won and the Left lost.

RIGHT: During the 1984 dispute, a network of several hundred miners' support groups were set up, often led by miners' "wives and girlfriends groups", such as Women against Pit Closures. But miners have not always been able to count on the sympathy of their other halves. The picture right shows miners' wives protesting in London against a threatened strike in September 1920.

ABOVE: London police apprehend a striking miner, June 1984.

RIGHT: Arthur Scargill, president of the National Union of Mineworkers, addresses miners at a rally in London, 1984.

222

BELOW: Miners gather outside the House of Commons during a march in Central London, October 1992.

United in Protest

In London the strike formed a bond between unlikely communities, all sharing one thing in common: a deep hatred of Thatcher and her government. At that year's Notting Hill Carnival, one of the most popular badges worn by partygoers read "Black people support the miners – oppose police violence".

1981 The Brixton Riots

It would be naively optimistic to declare race riots in London a thing of the past. In a city defined by its multicultural make-up, the potential for racial unrest remains a perennial, if distant threat.

In 1981, the south London district of Brixton was the scene of the most significant outbreak of civil disorder in 20th-century London. It was an area of high unemployment, particularly amongst its large Afro-Caribbean community, and also suffered from a high crime rate. In April that year, almost 1,000 people – mostly young black men – were stopped and searched on the streets of Brixton as part of a police initiative called "Operation Swamp".

The blue touch paper was lit on 13 April, when a rumour circulated that the police were trying to arrest an injured black man, rather than take him to hospital. Buildings were burnt and mass looting quickly took hold. By the time hostilities ceased, over 360 people had been injured and 28 premises burned. The total number of arrests was 82.

A government report into the riots was heavily critical of the Metropolitan Police, and prompted new thinking about policing, recruitment and training. But the Broadwater Farm riots in Tottenham four years later – with more unrest in Brixton occurring the same year – was a sharp reminder of the brittle nature of London's ethnic coexistence.

OPPOSITE BELOW: Policemen with riot shields form a cordon during the Brixton riots, April 1981.

LEFT: A boarded-up shop in Brixton advertises a "riot sale" in the months after the trouble, July 1981.

BELOW: An exhausted policeman rests on the kerb as a fire burns behind him after race riots erupted in Southall, west London, July 1981.

"The Brixton Black Panther Movement was not a separatist organisation like the Nation Of Islam. We didn't believe in anything like that. Our slogan was 'Black Power – People's Power'…"

Linton Kwesi Johnson, poet and former member of the Brixton
Black Panther Movement

ABOVE: Members of the Brixton Black Panther Movement carry banners through Paddington during an anti-police protest march in Notting Hill, August 1970. The Movement, inspired by the ideology of the US Black Panther Party, were active in London during the early 1970s.

LEFT: A policeman cautions two Sikh motorcyclists for not wearing crash helmets, September 1973. The motorcyclists were due to participate in a 3,000-strong procession through London with banners saying "Wearing crash helmets over turbans is not practicable."

Sexual Politics

The lives of gay Londoners has changed dramatically over the last quarter of the 20th century. Decriminalization of homosexual acts in the late 1960s, and the subsequent campaign for full legal parity with heterosexuals, helped build a sense of community and common purpose amongst gay people in the capital. Whilst homophobia still exists as a social concern, the eradication of government-approved discrimination against homosexuals is testament to the country's progressive instincts.

LEFT: A campaigner holds a placard at a Gay Liberation march in Oxford Street, circa 1975, calling for homosexual acts to be legalized for 16-year-olds – the same age as heterosexuals. The Sexual Offences Act 1967 had decriminalized homosexual acts, but only for males over the age of 21.

227

1958 London to Aldermaston

In 1958, London became the departure point for a political march that reflected a new fear: that of nuclear conflict. The London to Aldermaston rally was organized by the Campaign for Nuclear Disarmament (CND), whose ultimate aim was the global abandonment of nuclear weapons. The 52-mile march to Aldermaston's Atomic Weapons Establishment, which designs and maintains Britain's nuclear deterrent, attracted substantial attention. It was attended by people from all sections of society, including scientists, religious leaders, students, journalists, actors, musicians, trade unionists and left-leaning politicians such as Tony Benn and Michael Foot (both pictured on this page).

The march was replicated annually until 1965, although the route was switched so that it started in Aldermaston and finished in London. Despite their popularity, the marches had little political influence. Rather it was global events such as the Cuban Missile Crisis of 1962 that delivered the impetus for a softening of international policies. After the Missile Crisis was resolved, a ban on nuclear testing was agreed between the US, the Soviet Union and Britain.

A relaxing of global tensions over the immediate threat of nuclear war resulted in a dwindling of CND support. From the mid-1960s, nuclear issues began playing second fiddle to public anger over the United States' part in the Vietnam War. This paradigm shift in international politics further eroded the CND's presence. It continued to operate, with marches revived in 1972 and 2004, but as a much smaller movement.

ABOVE RIGHT: Two doyens of British liberal politics, Tony Benn (left) and Michael Foot (right), during a CND march from Aldermaston to London, March 1961.

RIGHT: Anthony Greenwood MP (third from right) and Tony Benn MP (extreme right) along with other supporters of nuclear disarmament wear sandwich boards advertising the Hydrogen Bomb Challenge to Mankind meeting, April 1954.

DOLCIS

STOP U.S. AGGRESSION IN VIETNAM

STOP U.S. ...OCITIES IN ...TNAM

STOP THE WAR

ABOVE: A demonstration in Central London against US involvement in the long-running Vietnam War, March 1968. The demo led to violence with 91 police officers injured and 200 demonstrators arrested.

RIGHT: Musician Billy Bragg (front) and politician Ken Livingstone at a demonstration against the first Gulf War, 1990.

229

1990 The Poll Tax Riots

In March 1990, the imminent Poll Tax, or Community Charge to give its official name, implemented by Margaret Thatcher's Conservative government, sparked mass disturbances across the UK. By far the largest occurred in Central London, around Trafalgar Square, leading to it being dubbed the modern-day Battle of Trafalgar. Hundreds were injured and arrested during the riots.

The unrest is considered by many a major factor in the political downfall of Margaret Thatcher, who resigned as prime minister in November the same year. Within months, her successor, John Major, announced the tax would be abolished.

RIGHT: A protester climbs a lamp post in Trafalgar Square holding a "Pay no Poll Tax" placard as a building burns in the background, March 1990.

BELOW: Placards are held aloft at a demonstration in Islington.

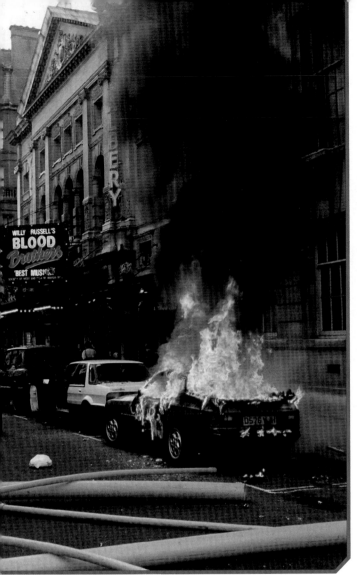

ABOVE: A demonstrator smashes a shop window close to Trafalgar Square.

LEFT: Burnt-out cars litter St Martin's Lane during the 1990 riots. Further down the street, Albery Theatre (now the Noël Coward Theatre) advertises a production of "Blood Brothers".

BELOW: A piece of wood thrown by a demonstrator in Trafalgar Square hurtles towards a police officer on horseback.

Milestone Moments

Significant events have often been marked with abundant pomp and ceremony in London. The presence of the Royal Family has given Londoners reason to congregate on the occasion of coronations, weddings and jubilees, while the arrival of peacetime in 1945 led to a symbolic spilling onto the streets of the city's joyous citizens. London has also staged major cultural and sporting events, including the Festival of Britain, two Olympic Games and a World Cup final, bringing the world's eyes onto the city and reinforcing its global standing.

BELOW: The golden state coach containing King George VI on the day of his coronation passes through Marble Arch toward Hyde Park as crowds cheer from the side of the road, May 1937.

"But it's all part of life's rich pageant"

Inspector Clouseau

A Ceremonial City

London's penchant for custom and ritual has remained constant throughout the 20th century, but its capacity for expression has been both curbed or enhanced at various moments.

Much of the city's ceremonial activities have revolved around the Royal Family, whose kings and queens have lived in the capital for almost 1,000 years. The city landmark most closely associated with the monarchy – and the scene for so much pageantry over the years – has been Buckingham Palace. Until 1993 the Palace was closed to the public, but when it eventually opened its doors to visitors, the change helped to bridge the divide between ordinary Londoners and its most famous family – not to mention creating a money-spinning tourist attraction.

No royal events have captivated Londoners as much as coronations. When Elizabeth II ascended the throne after the death of her father, King George VI, in 1952, she became the 39th sovereign to be crowned at Westminster Abbey. Some 3 million people lined the streets of London for the occasion, hoping to glimpse the new monarch as she travelled the four-and-a-half-mile route between Buckingham Palace and the famous cathedral. The coronation received extensive media coverage, with the BBC setting up its biggest-ever outside broadcast – in 44 languages – to provide live coverage. An estimated 27 million people in Britain watched the ceremony on television (at a time when only 2 million people owned televisions), whilst another 11 million listened on the radio.

Public gatherings in London at times of national celebration have not always been such mass communal affairs. Self-contained street parties also have a long history in the capital, dating back to 1919 and the end of the First World War, with the tradition of Londoners closing off their street, hanging up red, white and blue bunting, and enjoying a "knees up".

However, the opportunity for Londoners today to enjoy such occasions has been restricted. Until the 1970s, local communities in London would often arrange impromptu outdoor jamborees, but nowadays dates must be agreed in advance, with some local councils even charging a fee for the privilege.

The ways in which Londoners commemorate the nation's participation in war has also changed throughout the 20th century. A cursory glance at the official schedule for the VE Day celebrations in 1945 offers a fascinating insight into the prevailing atmosphere of the time. The itinerary brimmed with merry entertainment, including a production of Shakespeare's *As You Like It* in Regent's Park, plus Punch and Judy shows and children's ballet. A city that just four years earlier had endured the horrors of the Blitz was able to put aside the haunting memories of its darkest hours to revel in a new peace.

Three years later, in 1948, the eyes of the world fell upon London once more as the city hosted the world's most popular sporting carnival, the Olympic Games. The entire country was still in the grip of post-war rationing; bombed buildings still littered the city. It was by no means an ideal time to be staging such a momentous event and, with the nation on its knees, the decision was made to keep costs to a bare minimum. No new buildings would be constructed, and no dedicated accommodation would be laid on for athletes. The "Austerity Olympics" would end up costing just £600,000 to stage.

Responding to adversity, thousands of Londoners threw in their lot as volunteers and that year's Olympics became the first to feature volunteer participation on any significant scale. Entire communities simply turned up and pitched in: competitors from abroad lodged in the houses of volunteer families, boy scouts delivered cups of tea to athletes in the stadium, and both participants and spectators were driven to the venues in whatever vehicles could be laid hands on – including cabs, buses, trucks and military vehicles.

As London prepares to host its third Olympic Games in 2012, complete with glitzy, ultra-modern arenas and multibillion-pound sponsorship and advertising deals, it offers a stark contrast with the enforced amateurism of 1948. It also reminds us of the malleable qualities of the city and its people whenever London is required to stand tall and adopt a ceremonial pose.

ABOVE AND LEFT:
Illuminations at the Festival
of Britain site, 1951.

Royal Abode

The history of Buckingham Palace dates back more than 500 years, yet much of the building today is retained from the original structure built in the early 1700s. In 1837, Queen Victoria became the first monarch to take up residence at the palace, and a series of extensive changes followed, including the transportation of the huge arched gateway to Tyburn, where it remains today, known as Marble Arch.

Like so many London landmarks, the Palace was a major target for bombings during both World Wars, as the Germans set about eroding the nation's spirit. Despite several attempts, the venerable building emerged relatively unscathed, and if anything the experience served to strengthen the resolve of the people. This bond was further intensified in 1993 when the Royal Family took the decision to open the Palace to the public.

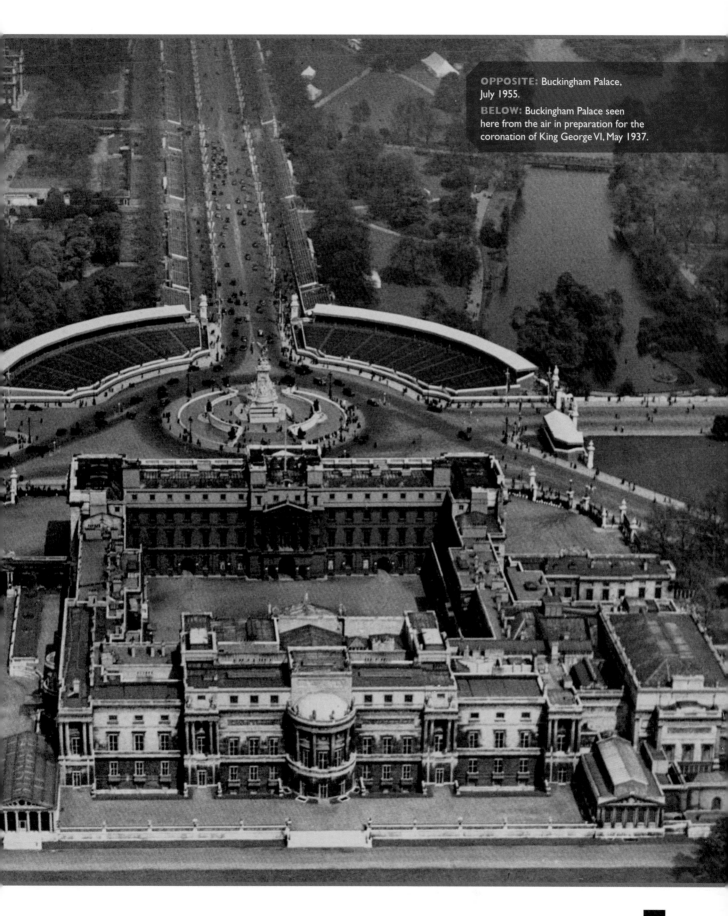

OPPOSITE: Buckingham Palace, July 1955.

BELOW: Buckingham Palace seen here from the air in preparation for the coronation of King George VI, May 1937.

Pomp and Circumstance

The setting for momentous occasions in London has often been the city's historical buildings and institutions. Westminster Abbey has staged the coronation of nearly every British monarch since that of William the Conqueror in 1066. During the 20th century alone it hosted four coronations, each of which was fervently celebrated on the streets of London. The contrasting occasions of high-profile weddings and funerals have also given rise to dramatic scenes of mass communal emotion in the city.

OPPOSITE AND ABOVE: The coronation of Queen Elizabeth II, June 1953.

BELOW: St James' Street, London, decorated for the coronation of George V, June 1911.

ABOVE: The state funeral for Winston Churchill at St Paul's Cathedral, January 1965.

RIGHT: Crowds gather in Trafalgar Square for the Queen's Royal homecoming, circa 1950.

OPPOSITE: Queues along the Embankment as a cortege for King George VI's funeral passes through London, February 1952.

The Royal Tournament

The Royal Tournament was a large military pageant, held annually by the British Armed Forces. It began life at the Royal Agriculture Hall in Islington, north London, before moving to the Earls Court Exhibition Centre in southwest London in 1950.

The tournament involved a series of competitions and ceremonial traditions performed by members of the British Army. It attracted increasing numbers of spectators as more crowd-friendly events were added to the roster, including music and rides. The tournament was eventually disbanded in 1999, however, after a government defence review deemed it too expensive. It was re-established in 2010 as the British Military Tournament, without the royal patronage it had previously enjoyed.

ABOVE: The RAF Falcon parachute display team publicize the Royal Tournament at Earls Court, July 1979.

OPPOSITE: The Royal Tournament, May 1936.

Britain goes to War

Before the days of 24-hour rolling news and television sets in almost every household, Londoners would gather for momentous events on the streets, rather than observe from the comfort of their living rooms. The thirst for instant news was quenched by crowds congregating at London landmarks, where information would filter through via official statements and radio broadcasts. The beginning of the Second World War saw Londoners flock to Downing Street where they waited with anticipation for confirmation that war had commenced.

LEFT: Passers-by look at a tailor shop window plastered with copies of the *Daily Mirror*'s "Wanted" poster for Adolf Hitler.

OPPOSITE: Large crowds gather outside the Houses of Parliament awaiting news of Britain's declaration of war on Nazi Germany, September 1939.

OPPOSITE: A victory march passes along the Mall towards Buckingham Palace at the end of the First World War, July 1919.

LEFT: Prime Minister Winston Churchill (centre) joins Princess Elizabeth (far left), Queen Elizabeth (second left), King George VI (second right) and Princess Margaret (far right) on the balcony at Buckingham Palace on VE Day.

BELOW: Soldiers stand alongside one of the bronze lions in Trafalgar Square during VE Day.

BELOW: Families at a street party to celebrate VE day, May 1945.

OPPOSITE ABOVE: A man dressed up as Hitler in a pub in Lambeth, south London, during VE Day celebrations, May 1945.

OPPOSITE BELOW: A reveller washes his face in a Trafalgar Square fountain during VE Day.

LONG ST

1908 The First London Olympics

Modern-day Olympic Games are notorious for the kind of political manoeuvring and financial burden that go hand-in-hand with staging the world's most famous sporting carnival. Yet a glimpse back at the 1908 Olympics, hosted by London, soon shows that it was ever thus.

Far from being a platform of virtue for the world's elite sportspeople to display their talents, the Games that year were tainted by ceremonial ineptitude, accusations of cheating and financial suspicion. Even the awarding of the Games to London was a hastily arranged affair that happened in dubious circumstances. Italy had withdrawn as hosts after the eruption of Mount Vesuvius, but many believe that it was simply a face-saving exercise to disguise the fact that they could not afford to stage the event.

And then there was the athletics themselves. The American Team alone lodged an average of one official protest a day, with their complaints ranging from the length of the running shorts to the ban on coaches entering the competition field.

The marathon was even more controversial. Canadian aborigine Tom Longboat collapsed after 19 miles, leading to claims by his Team that he had been drugged. Out of the shadows came Italian Dorando Pietri to lead the race all the way to the White City Stadium – an arena built in west London specifically for the Games.

Heat, exertion, and possibly the brandy he had been given, combined to make Pietri collapse five times and run the wrong way in the final stages. A posse of officials helped the exhausted runner over the line, leading to another US official complaint. This was upheld and Pietri's gold was given to the second finisher, American Johnny Hayes.

Britain's medal haul? A table-topping 56 golds.

LEFT: Women competing in an archery contest at the White City Stadium in west London during the 1908 Olympic Games. Archery is one Olympic event that has stood the test of time, but others held in 1908, such as bicycle polo and the tug-of-war, seem unlikely to make a return to such an exalted stage.

ABOVE: One of the earliest Olympic dramas to be captured on film. Dorando Pietri collapses after crossing the finishing line in the 1908 Olympic Marathon.

White City Stadium

Built in just 10 months, specifically for the 1908 Olympics by master builder George Wimpey, White City Stadium was big enough to accommodate 130,000 people with all its seating removed. Located in Shepherds Bush, west London, the stadium later became a popular venue for dog racing and speedway, as well as being home to Queens Park Rangers football club. It was demolished in 1985, to be replaced by BBC White City television offices.

1948 The Austerity Olympics

Taking place in an era of post-war rationing, the second London Games took on the epithet of the Austerity Olympics. With no money for the construction of new stadiums, events were held in ready-made venues instead – rowing at Henley, yachting at Cowes, and of course athletics at the famous old Wembley Stadium. In another sign of the times, building an Olympic village was deemed too expensive, so athletes were instead housed in no-frills accommodation, including RAF camps and colleges.

As for the fans, the mood of post-war patriotism had demonstrably carried over into the Games. Despite British athletes failing to replicate their 1908 success, managing only three gold medals between them, more than 80,000 spectators a day turned up at Wembley to cheer on their countrypeople.

LEFT: Female competitors in training at the 1948 London Olympics.

BELOW: Sprinters strain to cross the finishing line in the 100 metres event. The race was won by American athlete Harrison Dillard.

1951 The Festival of Britain

The Festival of Britain was intended to raise the nation's spirits after the devastation of war, whilst promoting the best of British art, design and industry. The layout of the site, centred around London's south bank, was meant to showcase the principles of urban design that would feature in the post-war rebuilding of the capital. Most of the buildings constructed for the Festival were International Modernist in style, an approach little seen in British architecture before the war.

However, despite the resounding success of the event, all of the new buildings except the Royal Festival Hall were later destroyed, including most controversially the Dome of Discovery, which sits prominently in the photo below left. The site of the Dome, which housed galleries and exhibitions dedicated to the theme of discovery, is now the location of the Jubilee Gardens.

ABOVE: An aerial view of the South Bank site of the Festival of Britain, 1951.
OPPOSITE ABOVE: The Royal Festival Hall on London's South Bank, built as part of the Festival of Britain celebrations.
OPPOSITE BELOW: Another view of the Festival site.

Bibliography

The following texts have been quoted, referred to, or used for research:

Books

Peter Ackroyd: *London: The Biography* (2001)

Jerry White: *London: The Story of a Great City* (2010)

Jerry White: *London in the 20ᵗʰ Century* (2008)

Michael H. C. Baker: *London Transport during the Blitz* (2010)

Barry Miles: *London Calling* (2010)

Time Out Guides: *London Through a Lens* (2008)

Time Out Guides: *Londoners Through a Lens* (2009)

Websites

http://www.20thcenturylondon.org.uk/

http://www.museumoflondon.org.uk

http://www.britainexpress.com

http://www.cityoflondon.gov.uk/

http://www.london-rip.com/

Acknowledgments

I would like to express my gratitude to those who saw me through this book; to all those who offered comments and suggestions, and assisted in the editing, proofreading and design.

Thank you to Richard Havers and Jeremy Yates-Round at Haynes Publishing for their vote of confidence and for their help and support throughout; to David Scripps, Alex Waters and the Mirrorpix team for their painstaking photographic archaeology that helped unearth so many of the wonderful pictures within these pages; to Robert Elms for penning the foreword, for the enthusiasm with which he set about the task, and for his ceaselessly brilliant radio show; to the various people who offered ideas, information and memories, all of which lend colour and texture to the book.

Special thanks to Adam McDonald, Anna Chapman, Vivienne Giddings, Joel Seager and Lydia Howland.

For Jodie.